AMERICA'S WOODEN AGE:
Aspects of its Early Technology

In this stand of virgin hardwoods, the large trees are white oak, which was one of the most important resources for America's Wooden Age. Courtesy: U.S. Forest Service.

AMERICA'S WOODEN AGE:
Aspects of its
Early Technology

Edited by Brooke Hindle

SLEEPY HOLLOW RESTORATIONS

TARRYTOWN · NEW YORK

Library of Congress Cataloging in Publication Data
Main entry under title: America's wooden age.
Bibliography: p.
Includes index.
1. *Technology—History—United States.*
2. *Wood-working industries—United States—History.*
3. *Waterpower—United States—History.*
I. *Hindle, Brooke.*
T21.A59   609'.73   74-7842
ISBN 0-912882-15-8

For information, address the publisher:
Sleepy Hollow Restorations, Inc.
Tarrytown, New York 10591

ISBN 0-912882-15-8
Library of Congress Catalog Card Number: 74-7842

First Printing

Printed in the United States of America

Designed by Ray Freiman

Sleepy Hollow Restorations, Incorporated, is a nonprofit educational institution chartered by the *Board of Regents of the University of the State of New York*. Established under an endowment provided, in large part, by the late John D. Rockefeller, Jr., Sleepy Hollow Restorations owns and maintains *Sunnyside*, Washington Irving's picturesque home in Tarrytown; *Philipsburg Manor, Upper Mills*, in North Tarrytown, an impressive example of a colonial commercial mill complex and *Van Cortlandt Manor*, in Croton-on-Hudson, a distinguished eighteenth-century family estate.

CONTENTS

ILLUSTRATIONS

Introduction: The Span of the Wooden Age

Brooke Hindle

THE TERM "Wooden Age" can be applied to a very long span of history during which man's dependence on wood was ubiquitous, not only in America but throughout the countries of Europe from which settlers came. It long preceded the first American colonies and it faded away only gradually. The primacy of wood as a material and as a fuel lasted longer in America than, for example, in Britain. In this country, a technology broadly based upon wood and a society pervasively conditioned by wood persisted until the mid-nineteenth century, when wood began, selectively, to be replaced by a rising utilization of other substances.

Much, then, of America's reliance on wood was shared with Europe generally and in particular with Britain and Ireland, the lands from which the great bulk of immigrants came during this period. On the other hand, there was a very important difference which rested almost entirely upon the vast plenty of wood in America. This contrasted markedly with the depletion of wood which in England itself had become serious as early as the thirteenth century. Before American settlement began, England had been so denuded of trees that the American contrast had many dimensions of significance.

Historians have long been sensitive to the similar contrast between the plenty of available land in America and its scarcity in Europe. Land has been well described as the greatest of the magnets which drew immigrants to America. Land had obvious economic significance—but it also determined political and social roles. Somehow the parallel importance of wood has not only escaped serious attention, but has even been egregiously misrepresented by some of the best historians.

Ultimately, the social meaning of wood—the manner in which it determined or influenced man's life in this country—may be its greatest significance. Wood, however, was connected to man and his life through his technology, his use of wood in making and doing things—almost all things. Before the social impact of wood can be delineated, man's wood-based technology must be understood; all else rested upon this.

This book seeks to open to view aspects of the technology of the Wooden Age and of the ways of wood. The essays represent selective probes into some of the most important sections of the panorama of wood. Each is presented, however, primarily because its author is currently at work upon the topic of which he writes. The authors are members of a small group of fine scholars who take the technology of wood seriously and are in a position to examine it with specific expertise as well as a sense of its broad meaning. This entire area of study is only now coming to maturity.

The viewpoint of this book is that the first need is to develop a sensitivity to the ways of wood. This sensitivity cannot be fully conveyed in a written paper because the three-dimensional world of wood has important nonverbal aspects which can be apprehended only by seeing, or even by touching, the objects involved. This is the reason for the inclusion of so many illustrations.

Wood was a wonderfully versatile substance which, in the period under consideration, was applied for the most part to three different uses: material, fuel, and processed chemical.

Its use as a material is the most obvious. It served in building houses, barns, and public buildings. It was used in constructing waterwheels and windmills, including their machinery. Ships, boats, wagons, bridges, railroads, and even canals and roads were built of it. Furniture, household wares, and many tools and operating devices were made wholly or partly of wood. Clocks and scientific instruments and even busts and statues were fabricated of wood.

As a fuel, wood was the basic resource for cooking and space heating. From it charcoal for the smelting of iron ore and the forging of iron was obtained. With the coming of the steam engine, it was the fuel first used in steamboats and locomotives.

Wood also provided the raw material from which important chemicals were derived. Potash, for example, was an early industrial alkali made from it. Naval stores, including pitch, tar, turpentine, and wood alcohol were obtained from coniferous woods. Bark was the source of tannin for tanning leather and the origin of certain dyes. Even maple sugar was extracted from trees.

American forests were not as they are sometimes pictured; they did not constitute a total expanse of primeval woodland, unbroken until the advent of the white man. The Indian had been here first and, together with the uncontrolled forces of nature, had been responsible for many and large clearings in grass, undergrowth, and other states of growth. Some were under cultivation or even recently burned out. Nevertheless, most of the eastern terrain was covered by a magnificent climax forest. Charles F. Carroll, whose article is an outgrowth of a broader study, recently published, shows very clearly the nature of this forest in New England and the nature of the initial assault of the English upon it. They applied and developed a technology largely unfamiliar to them. As Professor Carroll indicates, the efforts of most men must initially have been deeply influenced by forests and by wood. The central importance of the environment of great forests upon the selection and development of technology and upon the character of American civilization itself is a great undeveloped theme of history.

Building was one of the most important of the various aspects of the growing and continuing interchange between man, his available resources of wood, and his ways of making and doing things. Here, as everywhere, Americans did not often seek to innovate. Their initial effort was only to transfer to this country those skills and methods of building which they had known. As a consequence, the advantages of brick or stone construction for public and town buildings were duly appreciated and early town ordinances prohibited construction in wood. Nevertheless, wood predominated throughout this era, especially in regions lacking good building stone or brick clay. Changes were made in response to the environment. For example, New Englanders found it necessary to add weatherboard where it would not usually have been necessary in England. For different causes, shingle and thatch roofs were widely used and the very familiar tile of the mother country became infrequent.

Large-scale innovations were unusual. The first effort was to build wooden houses in the fashion familiar across the Atlantic. Wigwams, and all manner of shanty buildings were also erected—and have universally disappeared. The log cabin, of course, was imported from northern Europe and served throughout the era on the forested frontier and even in more settled places. The regional variation and adaptation in log cabin and log house construction was extensive and identifies a very interesting American development. The most distinctive American innovation in wooden building was the balloon frame, introduced in 1833 in Chicago. This not only saved wood but, in common with a general tendency in American technology, required very little skill in construction and in addition permitted use of pre-sawed and cut lumber.

These developments are closely linked to the spectacular rise to leadership of American woodworking machinery, so well presented by Nathan Rosenberg, an economic historian with a deep concern for technology. This clearly rested upon America's overwhelming dependence upon and use of wood. Before its flowering, in the machine technology described by Professor Rosenberg, American adaptability and leadership had already been demonstrated in hand tools. The American ax evolved from European models into an elegant instrument, so well balanced and finely designed that with it a man could fell three times as many trees in the same time as with its English counterpart.

The sawmill, presented in a pictorial essay by Charles E. Peterson, a student of building and building technology, spanned the entire period also, ending with the development of the muley saw, the circular saw, and the machinery noted by Professor Rosenberg. In the colonial period, sawmills were widely dispersed; they were second in numbers only to the gristmills found generally at good waterpower sites.

Much could be written of the pervasiveness of wood in American domestic life; the extent of dependence upon wood in farming was truly phenomenal. Not only were houses, barns, outbuildings, wagons, and furniture made of wood, but much of this was often done by the farmer himself. Moreover, wood was pressed into service for many uses which in a less wooded land could have been taken care of by different materials. Wooden fences were the rule—even in glacial terrain. All sorts of containers were made of wood, from barrels, buckets, and tubs to baskets, and even mugs and bottles. Hinges, hooks, and all manner of tools were fashioned in wood.

Perhaps the most unfamiliar and unlikely application of wood was in the service of art and high craftsmanship. The artistry of America's cabinetmakers who produced creative designs out of a wealth of trade and practice is readily recognized. In their work, they followed European practice in importing rare woods, often from tropical places, but the bulk of their work was in American wood.

It is a brief step from cabinetmaking to clockmaking; at least clockmakers were used to having their clock cases made by cabinetmakers. However, the return to wooden wheelwork in clocks was made for the purpose of introducing interchangeable, mass-produced components. Wooden clocks proved the bridge between handmade brass clocks and mass-produced brass clocks—in which America took command of the field.

Silvio A. Bedini, a scholar who has studied scientific instruments extensively, details a still more exotic application of wood—to the making of mathematical or scientific instruments. This is a small but fascinating American story from the age of wood, and it was limited in its full development to a part of the country. Whether this was entirely a matter of the greater availability of wood may be doubted, since so little of it was required in each piece. More likely it stands as a commentary on the spilling over of widely pervasive acquaintance with wood and widely developed skills in its use.

Perhaps the highest flight of wood was in its use for the plastic arts. Its application to the making of commercial signs is fairly obvious. Most of these were flat, but three-dimensional figures must surely have been anticipated. This, however, probably depended upon the extensive market for ships' figureheads that was supplied by artists of varying talent. The best took the final step to sculpture as a means of expression. The medium may seem unimportant, but it is unlikely that Rush, McIntyre, and the Skillins would have become sculptors in wood except for the larger world of wood carving in which they matured their skills.

In this wooden world, the most important complex of wooden machinery, found throughout the rural regions and as the foundation of some centers of population, was the water-powered gristmill. Occasionally, wind-powered mills were used, especially in New York and parts of New England, but even then the mill and its gearing and transmission system were almost identical to the watermill. Charles Howell describes, with the inside knowledge of the miller, the details and even personality of these mills. They were a central expression and identification of the Wooden Age.

In shipbuilding, wood gave the Americans one of their great economic advantages over England and much of Europe. Much wood was shipped to England, most dramatically the broad arrow trees claimed for Royal Navy masts, but most of this resource was applied to building ships here. Because they were cheaper, American-built ships constituted one-third of those sailing under the British flag at the time of the Revolution; by 1855, the American merchant marine carried more tonnage than any other. Our overseas commerce and our naval power rested upon our plenty in wood. This enormous success spurred innovation and design achievements in its wake. The

Baltimore clipper, the great American frigates of the Barbary and 1812 wars, and the clipper ships are the best known of these achievements.

Wood also underlay riverboat construction and commerce. Throughout its youth, America had a deserved reputation for the worst system of roads and overland transportation possessed by any civilized country in the world. As a consequence, its river transport, based upon a fine river system, was enormously important. Many varieties of specialized boats were developed here to serve this need: the keelboats on the western rivers, the Durham boat—a low-draft, large capacity boat—and the Hudson River sloop among them.

When canals were introduced to supplement and improve upon the river system, wood was more prominent than in Europe. Not only were the boats of wood, but the Americans made their locks of wood—instead of brick or stone—and usually their feeders or aqueducts, in the form of inside-out canal boats. There was even one unfulfilled scheme of building canals on top of the ground, entirely of wood, thus avoiding the great costs of excavation.

Wood did not solve the problem of the very bad roads, but it was pressed into service in this cause. The corduroy roads of the colonial era were merely logs laid beside one another to provide a less treacherous but very rough surface. Plank roads were imported from Canada, and for a time companies proliferated which quickly built toll roads with a tolerably good surface of sawn planks. In cities, good surfaces were made by using the grain end of wood rounds or blocks.

America did not solve its internal transportation problem until the arrival of steam power. More than any other people, the Americans concentrated their ingenuity and energy upon the application of the imported steam engine to transportation—first to steamboats and then to railroads. The first sustained success with steamboats was attained here. The very rapid development of specialized types of boats, different on the western rivers from the eastern, provided remarkable freight and passenger transportation. The boats, of course, were built of wood, but more important, they depended upon a readily available supply of wood for fuel. The cheap and ready supply of wood at the time of the introduction of the steamboat was a primary factor in its success and spread.

Similarly, railroads rested in the same way upon wood. The English practice of placing rails upon stone blocks was immediately abandoned in favor of wooden ties or sleepers; wherever the early railroads were built, the proximity of wood for ties proved a significant advantage. Locomotive frames, like stationary steam engine frames, were first made here of wood instead of metal. More striking, the early English locomotives imported to run the trains were converted from coal to wood burners and American-built locomotives were initially wood burners. The extension of railroads resulted from the same ready supply of wood fuel that spurred steamboat construction.

Railroads here boasted a much lower construction cost per mile than the English standard; a primary reason for this was the reliance upon wood for spanning rivers and valleys—instead of stone. This was doubly important because of the roughness of the American terrain. As a result of the extensive railroad building, America leaped to leadership in the design of truss bridges, a process which had begun even before the railroad era. For a time the goal of patenting a new and better design for wooden truss bridges became one of the get-rich-quick dreams in this country.

Wood as a fuel was a major factor in the development of both steamboats and railroads; it also played a part in the rise of stationary steam engine use. In this sense, therefore, both steampower and waterpower were developments of the Wooden Age—although the usual view is that waterpower belonged to the wooden past but steam to the future of coal and iron. Louis C. Hunter, best known for his study of steamboats, makes an original contribution in his constrast of steam with waterpower which reverses many of the old clichés.

Iron too, appearances to the contrary, was an integral part of the American age of wood. Here again, it was wood used as a fuel that was the inescapable ingredient. When iron first began to be produced in America, the universally used process required three ingredients: iron ore, wood for charcoal, and limestone for flux. England's depletion in wood threw her iron production into serious difficulty—a difficulty solved by a technological solution, the substitution of coke for charcoal. This change did not have to be introduced into America where wood abounded, and, since charcoal iron was superior to coke iron in quality, it would not be introduced for reasons of product improvement. For a time, just before the Revolution, America produced more iron than the mother country, but thereafter England moved ahead rapidly on the basis of the coke revolution combined with the introduction of rolling and puddling processes. This made American iron production archaic until the 1830s and 1840s when puddling and rolling began to be introduced and smelting by raw anthracite took precedence for a time before the large-scale conversion to coke. The iron story is particularly interesting because this is one of several instances in which America's plenty of wood caused her to lag technologically.

Wood as a fuel was most widely and generally known in terms of cooking and space heating. In England, because wood was scarce, space heating was expensive, with the result that many lived uncomfortably. In America, wood was initially free for the taking and remained so for a large proportion of the rural population. Before very long, its price rose sharply in the cities, but new standards of comfort had already been established. Because of the plenty of wood, Americans built enormous and wasteful fireplaces and expected to keep themselves reasonably warm in winter. This pattern lay distantly behind such achievements as the Franklin stove, the Rumford fireplace, and the various Nott stove improvements.

The use of wood as a substance was the foundation of America's chemical industry. The resources of wood led the English to encourage the early production here of potash, which depended wholly upon wood ashes as its raw material. Naval stores were similarly encouraged, with even more growing success. Overseas commerce and naval power depended upon the ready availability of tar, pitch, and turpentine which could only be obtained from extensive stands of coniferous trees. Leather tanning was another industry of the most extensive importance depending entirely upon a source of tannin, of which oak bark was the most readily available. Here once again, America was blessed with resources which made possible another industry—while England suffered from her lost forest resources. Other barks were used as dyes or as drugs, sometimes on shaky evidence.

America's Wooden Age was a wonderful era, specifically because of the nature of the prevailing technology which depended so heavily upon wood. The ubiquity of wood marked this as a peculiarly favored land, where, in the hand technology of the colonial era and in the machine technology of the early national era, the plenty of wood made significant differences. Americans used wood prodigally, as a fuel and as the chief material from which they fabricated their buildings, their transportation systems, and most of their technology. It may have been a source of their readiness to change and replace older methods or designs with new. It may have been a source of higher levels of expectation—in almost all material matters. In the Wooden Age, America began her ascent to industrial primacy and to the highest standard of living in the world. Wood was important as an ingredient in these developments. This book provides access to some of the ways of wood; the enthusiasm of the age can be apprehended from the enthusiasm of the authors, who share it.

The Forest Society of New England

Charles F. Carroll

Americas Wooden Age began long before the era of European exploration and settlement, for it was the Indians who first encountered the great deciduous and coniferous forests that covered so much of the land. For thousands of years Indian forest-dwellers eked out a meager existence by hunting, fishing, and gathering roots and berries in the shade of giant trees. They fashioned tools, buildings, and utensils from the products of the woodlands. They tapped trees for sweet nourishment and burned them to survive the wind and cold. Traveling along shaded waterways in canoes of logs or bark, they hunted woodland animals for food and clothing. They healed the sick with the salicin of the willow and the tannin of the oak, and fashioned wooden splints to mend their broken bones. When European settlers arrived in the seventeenth century and stood in awe amidst the trees, they learned much about life in the wilderness from America's ancient forest people.[1]

But if the Indians initiated America's Wooden Age, the early settlers of New England, more than any other group of European immigrants, brought this age to fruition. It was the New Englanders who adapted themselves quickly to woodland ways, applied advanced technology to forest industries, and produced forest products for distant peoples. The Indians had lived in harmony with nature, and they had used the woodlands and its creatures in order to survive. The New England axmen assaulted nature; and in the clash between man and the wilderness, both man and the land were transformed.

The great majority of the early settlers of New England were

13

Puritans who swarmed onto her shores during the 1630s. Coming primarily for religious reasons, they believed that the dissolution of Parliament in March 1629 meant that all hope for religious reform had faded away and England was entering "evil and declininge tymes." They truly believed that they had to embrace a "wilderness condition" for the sake of their immortal souls.[2]

But few men came to New England solely for the sake of religion. Most pioneers who settled north of the Merrimack during the early years of the seventeenth century were members of the Church of England, and their prime motive for emigration was economic opportunity. Even the most sincere Puritans who settled in southern New England had pondered over their immediate temporal condition in England as well as their eternal destiny.

It was often the American forest and its potential riches that lured Englishmen across the sea, for the very existence of seventeenth-century European society depended on timber and timber products. Until the axmen felled trees most craftsmen could not follow their callings; crops could be neither sown nor harvested; houses could be neither built nor furnished; clothes could not be made; bodies could not be warmed; ships could not sail; rivers could not be crossed; the fires of industry could not burn; wars could not be fought; and the sick could not be healed.[3]

And, if Puritans found themselves in the midst of a religious crisis, they were experiencing a timber crisis as well. For at a time when the English economy was expanding and English sea power was increasing, the nation was running out of trees. During the reign of Charles I there were few woodland tracts that covered more than 20 square miles of English countryside; and in some regions, particularly in the southeast, there were no trees save for those in the hedgerows (the narrow belts of woodland that were left for windbreaks and boundaries between pastures and between cultivated fields).[4]

As early as the winter of 1623–24, long before John Winthrop thought of leaving England, he had pondered over "the

Common scarcitie of woods and Tymber in most places of this Realme." The poor in this wood-starved society, he noted, continually chopped at young trees and hedges, and even at gates and bridges, and this practice discouraged landowners from practicing conservation. In the borough of Sudbury in Winthrop's native Suffolk—a town that was to send more immigrants to New England than any other in all of East Anglia—there was constant trouble over wood fuel and fuel prices all during the 1620s. Although the burgesses attempted to limit the use of firewood, no satisfactory solution to the timber crisis could be found.[5]

Thus, Englishmen read the reports of the forest resources of New England with great interest, and many found the wilderness inviting. John White, an indefatigable promoter of religious and economic enterprises who played a prominent part in sustaining the small Massachusetts settlements of the 1620s, was fully aware of the advantages of an abundant wood supply. Sir John Eliot, the eloquent Puritan Parliamentarian, stressed the opportunity for "making pitch, tarr, pottashes, and soap ashes," and for cutting trees for masts. And those "good spies," Samuel Skelton and Francis Higginson, who organized the first Congregational Church at Salem in 1629, greatly encouraged prospective settlers. After surviving a bitter New England winter, they sent letters to their fellow Puritans telling of "the prosperous good hand of Providence," and one commentator reveals that these reports were "sweeter, and more welcome to their principals in England than the grapes of Eschol were to Israel of old." Everything in the New England forest fascinated Master Higginson—even the squirrels that "by a certain skill will fly from tree to tree, though they stand farre distant"—and he sent back glowing reports of a verdant land rich in economic opportunity.[6]

The Puritan colonists who reached the New England coast in mid-June 1630 found both weather and season favorable for settlement. Unlike the Pilgrims who had arrived in Provincetown Harbor in November 1620 and found all nature standing with a weather-beaten face, the Puritan band encountered

a lush, green forest landscape. Along the shore, the strawber-
ries were beginning to ripen; and the air was richly scented
with the fragrance of cedar, pine, and spruce; indeed, when a
westerly wind prevailed, the aroma of these conifers reached
far out to sea.[7]

Governor Winthrop and other officials of the Massachusetts
Bay Company would have preferred the formation of one
settlement, but because Salem and Charlestown were already
settled and thousands of new settlers already on the way, such a
plantation was not practical. Therefore, after preliminary surveys, the settlers spread along the coast and headed into the
interior, establishing Medford, Watertown, Roxbury, Dorchester, Lynn, and Boston before the coming of winter. Before
the end of the decade, new arrivals—settlers with wanderlust
as well as political and religious fugitives—had founded many
towns in eastern Massachusetts, in the Connecticut Valley, in
Rhode Island, and along the Connecticut coast. Some Puritans
moved north beyond the Merrimack and founded Hampton
and Exeter; others mingled with the Anglican colonists along
the Piscataqua River.[8]

Almost all of the Englishmen who took part in the Great
Migration were forced to begin a new life in the forest. And
those who arrived during the summer must have found the
woodlands even more dangerous, mysterious, and frightening
than the bleak and leafless outer Cape that the Pilgrims had
encountered. For the branches of the great trees towered over
the land and often blotted out the direct rays of the sun,
creating an unfamiliar and often eerie scene. Many believed
that hordes of Indians—a race of men "transformed into
beasts"—lurked in the shadows, and every strange and unfamiliar disturbance, every weird and wild outcry, every discharge of a musket was the occasion for alarm, for the call to
arms, for the doubling of the watch. The settlers encountered
the temptingly beautiful poison sumac and poison ivy, and
blood ran down their limbs as they were cut by the brambles,
bushes, and thorns. The croaking of frogs, the chirping of
crickets, the squalling of jays, the lonesome tones of the noc-

turnal whippoorwill, and the hideous and bloodcurdling sounds of wolves and cougars filled them with fear. And the rattlesnake, with a sting so deadly that it can kill a grown man in an hour, was so terrifying that some returned immediately to the safety of England.[9]

For those who remained, however, it was not the Indians, animals, and reptiles but the insects that caused the greatest suffering. In the spring and early summer the colonists were plagued by buffalo gnats in swarms so thick that a man could not draw his breath without sucking them in. And, as summer approached, large biting and blood-sucking flies appeared, especially where there were cattle. Many settlers also complained of the ticks that attached themselves to their garments and even crept into their breeches "eating themselves in a short time into the very flesh." But in summer it was the clouds of gnats and mosquitoes, hovering over the settlements, that were the most annoying of all. Many Englishmen were stung with such frequency and ferocity that their faces were "swell'd and scabby" as if they suffered from smallpox.[10]

The first goal of every new settler was survival in this bug-infested wilderness. Unless large food supplies were brought from England, however, starvation was possible. For even though the forest was full of squirrels, deer, turkeys, pigeons, and other game, many settlers, especially the poorer sort, had never hunted nor fired a gun in England. During the winter of 1630–31, some settlers survived only on clams, acorns, and groundnuts until the arrival of supply ships in the spring.[11]

For those with adequate food supplies, shelter was the most important problem. Some poor settlers lived in tents during their first winter in New England, and a few were able to build Indian wigwams. But the dugout seems to have been the most common type of shelter built by new arrivals, and even some of the wealthiest settlers lived for a time in these wretched hovels. The dugouts were built by digging a hole in the earth, "cellar fasion," to a depth of six or seven feet, or sometimes by digging into the side of a hill. The breadth of the hole was determined by the needs of the builder's family, and after the digging was completed the excavation was covered over and lined with the trunks of small trees. Cracks were sealed with canvas and mounds of dirt, clay, and turf; but unless a sloped roof was built over the shelter there was little protection from heavy rain. The walls inside the dugout were often covered with bark, and sometimes the floor and ceiling were planked. It was impossible to keep such dwellings clean, however, and it is no wonder that many new immigrants took one look at how men lived in the New England forest and then took the next ship for home.[12]

Many men could not leave their homes of earth for wooden houses, Edward Johnson recalled, "till the earth, by the Lord's blessing, brought forth bread to feed them, their wives, and little ones." And because there was not nearly enough open land to distribute to all participants in the Great Migration, many were forced to clear sections of the forest before they could begin to cultivate the land.[13]

The Indians destroyed trees by girdling. They cut off the bark in a ring around the tree and planted corn, squash, and pumpkins beneath the leafless branches. The trunks and branches of the decaying trees were only gradually removed and used for firewood. Some colonists adopted Indian methods on some of their lands, but many settlers did not plant crops until they had removed all of the trees and dug out all of the stumps and roots. If the roots were not removed, the land was difficult to plow and harrow, and often it could be cultivated only with a spade or hoe.[14]

Hauling off trees and grubbing up roots was an extremely slow method of land clearing, especially in the hardwood forests, which provided the most fertile lands for agriculture. The unwieldy European felling ax used by the first settlers was unsuitable for such a great task. Its brittle iron head, weighing more than four pounds, often cracked when the weather was cold, and the thin steel blade welded onto the head had to be sharpened frequently and replaced periodically. It was only during the eighteenth century that a smaller, lighter, well-balanced felling ax came into general use in the American forests.[15]

The amount of land that could be cleared with the crude tools and small draft animals of the seventeenth century is uncertain. Wealthy colonists were able to hire men or use indentured servants to clear land between the fall harvest and the planting season. But most colonists could not afford such help, and they also engaged in many other essential tasks during the winter. Hard frosts and deep snows also impeded land clearing. There was a great "store of plowland" in Sudbury, Edward Johnson wrote in 1651, "but by reason of the oaken roots, they have little [ground] broken up, considering the many acres the place affords." All things considered, an inexperienced settler could not have cleared more than four or five acres of woodland a year. It was only by taking full advantage of natural clearings and abandoned Indian fields, and by engaging in an extensive form of forest husbandry, that the participants in the Great Migration managed to survive.[16]

In England, where the sheep was the predominant domestic animal, the hog was unimportant, for many families did not have enough kitchen waste to keep even one. Once they entered the North American forest, however, the immigrants found that the hog-sheep ratio of England was reversed, for sheep thrive only on open meadows and not in woodlands. Hogs, however, were originally woodland animals, and they are able to live on young shoots, roots, and the fruits and nuts that fall in abundance from the trees. The colonists discovered that the quantity of pork in the New England forest could be doubled every 18 months.[17]

But if hordes of hogs roaming through the woodlands were an essential food supply, they were often a menace. For they enjoyed feeding on corn as well as on wild fruits and nuts, and once they invaded the cornfields they could destroy a whole crop and endanger the very existence of a settlement. Because of this threat, the colonists soon learned that the construction of barriers around the fields was an essential part of agricultural labor in a wooded environment. They also found that barriers were often necessary to keep the wolves from the shoats, calves, and other young animals.[18]

In the counties of southern England where most of the settlers were born, husbandmen used ditches, hedges of hawthorn or privet or sedge, or high woven barriers called "hays" to enclose their fields. Timber was too scarce and valuable for use in fencing. During the growing season domestic animals were kept well away from the crops, and they did not need protection of any kind, for the land was tame and void of dangerous animals. But in the New England forest, Englishmen quickly recognized the necessity and practicality of a new type of barrier: the wooden fence. Such fences kept most roaming animals from the corn, and also kept the wolves from the cattle.[19]

Where the system of common fields prevailed, the building of wooden fences quickly became one of the most important community efforts. Most towns appointed fence viewers to ensure that the barriers were built properly and kept in repair. Nothing is more conspicuous in early town records than hog and fence regulations—and their violation. The wooden fences were continually mended, but sections were often in disrepair and the wandering hogs took advantage of the colonists' neglect and enjoyed a good meal of corn. The hogs were pests, the crops were always in danger, and farmers continually worried about their future in this new environment of grunts and squeals. Many must have longed for the pastoral English countryside. The number of sheep did increase in coastal New England as the land was cleared, but the hog remained the predominant farm animal of the advancing frontier.[20]

Many settlers left their wigwams, dugouts, and other makeshift shelters for more suitable living quarters only after they had cleared a portion of their land, planted crops, and built fences to keep out the roaming animals. The first houses did not, at first glance, reflect swift adaptation to a wooded environment. The log cabin would have been an ideal dwelling for the settlers of the New England forest. Such cabins can be built from coniferous trees by the use of the felling ax alone; they require less labor than other types of construction; and the builder does not need nails or other hardware. But Englishmen, coming from a region that was totally lacking in large conifers, were not familiar with such buildings. They continued to square oak logs with a broad ax and construct the traditional English frame dwelling.[21]

The frame of the traditional English dwelling was held together by notched joints and wooden pegs. The cutting of large notches weakened the framing timbers, and they could withstand the weight of the roof, walls, and chimneys only if they were very thick. Thus, the construction of even a small dwelling in New England required the cutting and hauling of tons of timber. The frames of such dwellings were troublesome to raise after they were pieced together on the ground, and it was difficult for builders to join the massive sections, especially when working on the second story or on the roof. Because insulation was necessary in such a cold climate the spaces between the studs had to be filled with handmade clay bricks, or with boughs woven into a lathing that would accept a filling of clay and straw or horsehair.

Although the early settlers followed traditional construction practices, they quickly made some changes because of the new environment. In England the outer walls of most dwellings were plastered and the roofs were thatched. In New England both walls and roofs were covered with boards, clapboards, or shingles. And fireplaces were much larger in the dwellings of the new forest society than in England, for the climate was much colder and the wood supply was seemingly limitless. Wooden barns and other outbuildings were also built much more frequently in New England than in the treeless English countryside. Indeed, barns were the largest structures built in Massachusetts and Connecticut during the Great Migration. Outbuildings, owned only by men of status in England, could be built by men of common means in the new woodland society.[22]

Men of common means also adopted a new form of transpor-

Snake and post-and-rail fences drawn by Luigi Castiglioni, an Italian visitor to the New World in the 1780's. From *Viaggio negli Stati Uniti dell America Settentrionale fatto negli anni 1785, 1786, & 1787* (Milan, 1790), 2 vols. Courtesy: John Carter Brown Library, Providence, R. I.

New England dwellings (above) framed in the traditional
English style, with notched joints and wooden pegs, as
reconstructed at Plimoth Plantation, Plymouth, Mass. This
photograph, and others not otherwise credited in this
chapter, were taken by the author.

tation in the forest: the canoe. Dugout and birchbark canoes, used by the Indians for centuries, were often the only means of travel in a wilderness drained by a multitude of small rivers and streams. Building large numbers of canoes during the 1630s, the settlers used them for ferries and for carrying such products as firewood, clay, thatch, and furs. Some adventurous souls, emboldened by the example of the Indians, even sailed these slender, unstable craft into the choppy waters of the sea. In such communities as Dedham and Salem canoe travel rapidly became a way of life. And canoes, like hogs, wooden fences, clapboard houses, blazing wood fires, and great barns gave evidence of the new forest society that was developing in New England.[23]

Skill in the use of the ax, land clearing, fence building, forest husbandry, canoeing, and modifications in building construction demonstrate the vigor of the new settlers in their struggle to adapt to a new environment. By 1640, when most immigration to New England ceased because of the intensifying struggle in England between Parliament and the Crown, thousands of New Englanders had adjusted to woodland ways. Now they were prepared to solve their economic difficulties by exploiting the forest riches of their newly adopted land.

The basic economic problem for New Englanders in the years after 1640 was the acquisition of essential manufactured articles, especially clothing and ironware (pots, pans, nails, weapons, tools, and cutlery). These were commodities that could not be produced efficiently in a pioneer society. Woolen cloth could not be manufactured in large amounts because large numbers of sheep could not find forage on uncleared lands. Iron could not be produced in large quantities because high labor costs totally offset the advantage of an abundant fuel supply. These essential goods could be obtained only by the development of an extensive trade.[24]

New England, however, had few products available for export. Although the sour and rocky soil produced some grain surpluses, few settlers were able to pay for all the manufactured goods they needed by selling agricultural products. Furs were easily transportable and brought high prices in European markets, but trappers had destroyed the most valuable fur-bearing animal, the beaver, in the coastal area by the mid-1630s, after which profits from the fur trade were enjoyed only by a favored few who, under government licenses, dealt with the Indians of the interior. And if an ocean rich in fish partially compensated for unfavorable conditions on land, most New Englanders knew nothing about salt-water fishing or the ways of the sea. Large export surpluses could not be produced by inexperienced seamen in one or two fishing seasons.[25]

New Englanders, therefore, had to turn to the forest in order to obtain products for immediate export. New England merchants were forced to scan the ports of the Western world in search of those who would purchase such commodities. Quickly the wine ports of Spain, Portugal, the Canaries, Madeira, and the Azores, all suffering because of diminishing timber supplies, became the first major markets of New England. And the white oak, which provided barrel staves and heading impermeable to wine but porous enough for air to filter through properly to control oxygenation, became the first important commercial tree of New England.[26]

English settlers who had attained some skill in lumbering while clearing the land now began to fell giant white oaks. They sawed the trunks into sections, and then cleaved boards along the radius of the logs with a beadle and frow. Sometimes these riven clapboards were exported in this crude form, but they were often shaved and shaped into pipe staves and even formed into casks by industrious coopers in Boston, Salem, and other seaside communities. The casks, once formed, were disassembled and shipped as prefabricated or "shaken" casks. The headings for the casks were pieces of white oak, and the hoops that bound the staves together were made from saplings of hickory and white oak or from willow branches.[27]

Before the end of 1640 a merchant-adventurer in Boston exported 8,500 pipe staves aboard an English vessel. And in 1641 that defiant Anglican of Noddles Island, Samuel Maverick, sent a shipment of staves to an English agent in

This detail of a building shows a corner post, girts, studs, and woven lathing.

Indian method of building a dugout canoe, shown right in a print from Theodore DeBry, *Admiranda Narratic Fida Tamen, de Commodis.* . . . (Francoforti Ad Moenum, 1590). Courtesy: John Carter Brown Library, Providence, R. I.

Girts and studs shown in detail.

Málaga, on Spain's Mediterranean coast. The agent sold Maverick's cargo, forwarding both Spanish money and fruit to a Bristol merchant, who, in turn, gave Maverick credit for English manufactures needed in New England.[28]

New Englanders found a second great outlet for their timber products in the markets of the West Indies. The British island of Barbados had been settled by many relatives and friends of the New England colonists; and in the mid-1640s some were developing sugar plantations along the coast. Tropical trees were falling before the axes of indentured servants and slaves, and as the woodlands were destroyed and the land planted in sugar and other crops, New England traders found a ready market in products essential for the survival of the island. Red-oak staves cut in the forests of New England made excellent barrels and chests for both white and brown sugar. Although red oak was more porous than white oak, it was probably more abundant, and it even could be used for containers of heavy molasses. New Englanders also were able to supply the planters with large oak timbers and shingles for houses, barns, storehouses, and sugarworks. And there was a market for the horses and hogs that ran wild in the New England forests. Most important of all, a great market developed for white-pine boards. Beginning in the late 1640s, thousands of feet of white-pine boards were shipped from Boston to Barbados, and to the less-developed sugar islands of Nevis, St. Christopher, and Montserrat. In return, New Englanders received either sugar or bills of exchange, and they used these items to buy needed manufactures in England.[29]

Because of the high cost of labor, the great demand for white-pine boards in the West Indies could not have been satisfied without the application of advanced technology to the lumber industry in New England. The up-and-down sawmill—a machine that transfers the power of flowing water into circular motion by use of a waterwheel and then into reciprocating motion by means of a crank—had been developed on the Continent by the fifteenth century. But there were few, if any, of these machines operating in England even in the seventeenth century. However, the English settlers imported this technology from Denmark and possibly from other nations of northern Europe. The first sawmill in New England was built in 1634 by English carpenters, assisted by Danish technicians, at John Mason's plantation on the Great Works River, near the present town of South Berwick, Maine.[30]

As the demands of the West Indian planters for boards increased, more and more sawmills were built along the streams of New England, especially in the region north of Cape Ann where safe harbors, navigable inland waterways, a steady stream flow, accessible white pines, and long-lasting snows combined to create the optimum environment for lumbering. Less than a dozen sawmills were built in this region prior to 1650, but by 1675 at least 50 mills—half of them in Maine—were in operation, many capable of producing several hundred thousand feet of boards a year.[31]

To complement the trade with the Wine Islands and the Caribbean, New Englanders opened a third great timber market in England. For even though London merchants and Yankee traders both discovered that the export of staves, boards, beams, and shingles across the Atlantic to England was unprofitable because of the great distance and high shipping costs, they developed a trade in masts and spars. These naval stores could be obtained at less cost in northern Europe, but in the seventeenth century the royal navy feared that an enemy nation might blockade The Sound (the strait between Denmark and Sweden at the entrance to the Baltic) and cut off supplies essential for the building and maintenance of men-of-war. In addition to the strategic advantages of an American trade, naval administrators also discovered an inherent advantage in New England masts. The white pines of New England may have been softer and less durable than the heavier northern European firs, but their size—sometimes over three feet in diameter and often 150–200 feet tall—allowed shipwrights to

Board warehouse at the Saugus Iron Works in Saugus, Mass. The boards are reproductions of those made at sawmills built along the streams of New England.

A dwelling, reconstructed at Plimoth Plantation, utilizing the common elements of seventeenth-century construction: vertical boards, steep pitched, shingled roof, and a square chimney at one end.

An up-and-down-sawmill, of the type commonly found in
New England, now operates at Upper Canada Village,
Morrisburg, Ontario.

install a single tree as a mainmast in the largest ships of the line. When European firs were used for this purpose a number of smaller trees had to be spliced.[32]

Thus, despite extremely high transportation costs, the New England mast trade flourished. As early as 1645 a number of Massachusetts traders posted a £1,000 bond, assuring four English merchants that they would prepare 100 masts, each between 16 and 36 inches in diameter, at Kennebunk, Maine. By the early 1650s many of the great white pines that lined the bays and rivers of northern New England were reaching the royal navy every year. And by the early 1670s Sir William Warren, the great English timber merchant, had over 250 New England masts, worth well over £35,000, stored in his timberyards at Wapping. By this time ten mast ships were departing from New Hampshire each year.[33]

The opening of the timber markets in the wine ports, the West Indies, and England had a significant effect on New England society. Lumbering became the full-time occupation of many settlers in the region north of Cape Ann, and many farmers in southern New England cut trees for staves and boards during the winter. Colonists who tilled the soil near heavily wooded swamps cut white-cedar logs, hewed them straight and true, and rived fragrant shingles in order to supplement their incomes. In Plymouth Colony some settlers made pitch and tar from the pines that thrived on the sandy soil of Cape Cod. In terms of shipping tonnage, timber and timber products were always the most important exports of New England in the seventeenth century. Although the fishing industry grew rapidly in the 1640s and the value of fish soon exceeded the value of timber shipped to the wine ports and possibly to the West Indies, fish never accounted for more than 25 percent of the total export tonnage of New England.[34]

The timber trade, therefore, was the major factor in the growth of the shipbuilding industry of New England. Stimulated by this growing trade with the wine ports during the 1640s, the industry developed rapidly in the region around Boston and Salem. More than a dozen vessels of 200 tons or more, and nine rated at 100 tons or more, were built in New England ports during the 1640s. After 1650 the shipping tonnage of New England continued to increase as more and more timber products were sent to the Wine Islands and the West Indies. There was, however, a dramatic decrease in the size of New England vessels, the average tonnage of a ship during the second half of the seventeenth century being somewhere between 40 and 50 tons.[35]

The frequent loss of large vessels and the development of the North American coastal trade partly accounted for the shift to smaller vessels. But the rapid growth of the West Indies trade was also a significant factor influencing the size of New England ships. For the relatively short distances in West Indian commerce, the seasonal nature of the trade, the relatively large number of small West Indian ports that could easily be glutted with cargo, and the lack of bulky products for return voyages meant that small vessels were essential if Yankee merchants were to earn maximum profits. In the seventeenth century New England shipwrights were seldom called upon to take full advantage of the giant oak and pine timbers that were so readily available.[36]

Trends in New England shipbuilding and the growth of shipping tonnage can be correlated closely with developments in the timber trade. And the pattern of the timber trade, in turn, can be correlated closely with important political developments in New England. For the demand for timber in the wine ports, the West Indies, and England was a major factor in the expansion of Massachusetts Bay.

Beginning in the early 1640s the Puritan merchants of Boston, Salem, and Ipswich made large capital investments in timberland and sawmills in the region north and east of the Merrimack. Once these investments were made, it was inevitable that these merchants would advocate the extension of the authority of the Massachusetts General Court over the entire area. For without a stable government in this vast forest region the merchants could not collect their debts nor safely continue to risk their capital.[37]

In 1641 the Massachusetts General Court brought Dover and Strawberry Bank (Portsmouth), New Hampshire, within its jurisdiction, and in 1643 it extended its authority over Exeter. This allowed the Massachusetts merchants to exploit more fully the vast storehouse of white oak that grew along some of the tributaries of the Piscataqua. And when the West Indian and English markets for white-pine products opened up later in the decade, and investments in sawmills began to grow in Maine as well as New Hampshire, additional political moves were considered essential. During the early 1650s the Massachusetts merchants, taking advantage of favorable political conditions in England, persuaded their legislators to declare that the royal patent set the northern boundary of the Bay Colony somewhere north of Falmouth (Portland), Maine. Gradually during this decade the towns of Kittery, York, Wells, Saco, Cape Porpoise, Scarborough, and Falmouth were joined to the Puritan commonwealth.

There is little doubt that the principal forces behind the expansion of Massachusetts northward were timber imperialists rather than religious imperialists, for the Massachusetts General Court guaranteed the settlers in New Hampshire and Maine—even the Baptists, Quakers, and Antinomians—religious freedom. And in the settlements north of the Merrimack where the population was large enough to warrant representation in the Massachusetts General Court, representation was granted without the application of the test of Congregational church membership that was required of all settlers who lived within the previous boundaries of the Bay Colony.[38]

By the seventh decade of the seventeenth century the exploitation of the woodlands of New Hampshire and Maine was so profitable that influential men in England were preparing to move in on the economy that Massachusetts merchants had steadily built up over the years. The commissioners sent by Charles II to New England in 1665 examined the economic potential of northern New England. However, they were unable to create governments independent of Massachusetts in that region, and in 1667 and 1668 the Bay Colony merchants and their allies in the General Court tried to appease the Crown by shipping masts prepared in the Piscataqua region to the royal dockyards.[39]

The challenge to the dominance of the Massachusetts merchants in New Hampshire and Maine became increasingly serious, however, by the eighth decade. In 1676 the Lords of Trade, seeking information on alleged violations of the Navigation Act of 1673, sent Edward Randolph to New England. Randolph's reports accusing some Massachusetts Bay Puritans of disloyalty to the Crown eventually led to the revocation of the charter of the colony in 1684. In the meantime, the Lords of Trade recognized Robert Mason's rights to the land in New Hampshire, and they also ordered the Massachusetts General Court to withdraw its claim of authority over that region. In 1679 a new royal government was created for New Hampshire, and despite the incompetency and corrupt policies of the first royal governor the colony was never again under the jurisdiction of Massachusetts Bay.[40]

Massachusetts was able to obtain a new royal charter in 1691, and she maintained her economic and political control over Maine. But Massachusetts retained some degree of power and independence only because the merchants and their allies in the General Court were willing to compromise and to cooperate with influential English groups who profited from the exploitation of the timberlands of Maine. Puritan society continued, but it was not the isolated society envisioned by the founding fathers who had fled England in fear that they would lose their souls.

The wilderness, in itself, did not change the Puritans or their objectives. Change did not come about because of quick and successful adaptation to one or even several features of the new forest environment. Land clearing, new methods of agriculture, lumbering, the adoption of the Danish sawmill and the Indian canoe did not, in themselves, change the direction of society. No man modified or lost his religious values by killing a wolf or a bear or by chopping down a tree. Yet the total system that emerged in New England—a system that joined the lumbermen of northern New England to the prosperous Massachusetts ports, and the merchants and craftsmen of those ports, in turn, to the complex social and economic systems of the British, French, Portuguese, and Spanish empires—ensured that the settlers, even the most pious Puritans, would become something other than they started out to be.

Entering the forest as neophytes in the years before the 1640s, the men and women of the treeless English countryside learned, by the cruel tests of trial and error, the methods of survival in a harsh and bitter land. Wealthy English landowners, and even some men of low degree, became timber merchants. Men accustomed to the hum of small commercial towns, or to the bustle of the great metropolis of London, overcame their fears of the sound—and the stillness—of the woodlands, and became experts at sending ten tons of pine or oak crashing to the forest floor. Husbandmen who had left patterned hedgerows and gently rolling pasture lands produced timbers for mighty ships, and their sons became apprentices to coopers and ship carpenters in the busy seaside towns. The builders of gristmills, accustomed to rotating gears, became experts on the reciprocating motions of the saw. And these merchants, lumbermen, and craftsmen together initiated America's Wooden Age.

America's Rise
to Woodworking Leadership

Nathan Rosenberg

I

O NE OF the greatest difficulties confronting the writer of economic history is to convey to his audience a full sense of the kinds of problems which plagued and confounded his ancestors. This is particularly so in a country such as the United States that prides itself upon its technological versatility and tackles the most spectacular technological problems with an exuberant—not to say brash—self-confidence. In a society which now routinely practices such arcane crafts as "molecular architecture" and "genetic engineering"—activities which put to shame the medieval alchemist who would have been satisfied merely to turn dross into gold—it requires a great mental leap to understand the limitations confronting the colonial craftsman or the early nineteenth-century machinist. In a society which takes for granted a remarkably wide range of substitutability among material inputs in the production process—indeed, whose members would be hard-pressed even to identify the materials composing their tabletops or sweaters—it is difficult in the extreme to appreciate the constraints confronting early Americans as they went about their ordinary productive activities. For our technological versatility is a recent acquisition—essentially a product of the past century or so. As we go farther back in historical time we enter a period in which one of the most distinctive characteristics was an extreme dependence upon the raw facts of the natural environment.

This dependence provides a central underlying theme of this

essay, concentrating upon the emergence of woodworking machinery in America between 1800 and the 1850s. Preindustrial societies—let us say America in 1800—were heavily dependent upon the particular combinations of raw materials presented by their environments. Their capacity to manipulate or transform these materials was extremely modest, and therefore the number of technological options open to them was typically very small. Furthermore, in a world of high transport costs, especially away from bodies of navigable water, most productive activities were dependent upon local resources within a very small radius. It is important also to emphasize the fact, obvious though it may be, that wood supplies were not abundant everywhere, and that supply conditions for any particular locality may have altered drastically over time.

An American builder in 1800 knew nothing of aluminum or prestressed concrete, nor was the textile manufacturer even dreaming of synthetic fibers. Their choices were, first of all, dictated by their small stock of technological knowledge and the severely restricted portions of the natural environment which could be made economically productive within the confines of that limited technology.

The constraints upon their productive activities, however, were not solely technological but economic as well. It was technologically possible in 1800 to produce a wide range of objects—e.g., machinery—out of either wood or iron. But, in America at least, although iron was a technologically feasible alternative, the retarded state of the iron industry rendered that material prohibitively costly in many uses. The extent of American dependence upon wood in the first half of the nineteenth century was a reflection of the economic fact that wood was a far cheaper raw material. The profusion of forest resources, therefore, must be seen as an environmental fact which significantly accelerated the industrial growth of the American economy, once Americans had developed appropriate techniques for their exploitation.

The extent of early American dependence upon wood is difficult to exaggerate. As the major source of fuel, the primary building material, and a critical source of chemical inputs (potash and pearlash),[1] it was a raw material par excellence. Lewis Mumford's assertion that "wood was the universal material of the eotechnic economy" was still true at the beginning of the nineteenth century. The following statement would also apply without serious modification to America in 1800:

> As for the common tools and utensils of the time, they were more often of wood than of any other material. The carpenter's tools were of wood, but for the last cutting edge: the rake, the oxyoke, the cart, the wagon, were of wood: so was the washtub in the bathhouse: so was the bucket and so was the broom: so in certain parts of Europe was the poor man's shoe. Wood served the farmer and the textile worker: the loom and the spinning-wheel, the oil presses and the wine presses were of wood, and even a hundred years after the printing press was invented, it was still made of wood. The very pipes that carried water in the cities were often tree-trunks: so were the cylinders or pumps. One rocked a wooden cradle; one slept on a wooden bed; and when one dined one "boarded." One brewed beer in a wooden vat and put the liquor in a wooden barrel. Stoppers of cork, introduced after the invention of the glass bottle, begin to be mentioned in the fifteenth century. The ships of course were made of wood and pegged together with wood; but to say that is only to say that the principal machines of industry were likewise made of wood: the lathe, the most important machine-tool of the period, was made entirely of wood—not merely the base but the moveable parts. Every part of the windmill and the water-mill except for the grinding and cutting elements was made of wood, even the gearing: the pumps were chiefly of wood, and even the steam engine, down to the nineteenth century, had a large number of wooden parts: the boiler itself might be of barrel construction, the metal being confined to the part exposed to the fire.[2]

The importance of wood in the American economy may be gauged in various ways. If American manufacturing industries are ranked by value added by manufacture in 1860, the lumber industry component of wood use alone ranks a close second behind cotton goods. Lumbering was the largest single manufacturing industry, on this basis, in the south and west.[3] Table 1 presents estimates of lumber consumption in the United States and compares them with estimates for the United Kingdom. Two propositions emerge clearly from the table, and deserve emphasis: (1) Per capita lumber consumption begins to rise in the 1820s and rises very sharply in the 1830s and after. (2) Per capita lumber consumption in the United States was several times as great as in the United Kingdom.

The second proposition should not be surprising. The United Kingdom in the early nineteenth century was much further along the road to industrialization than the United States. It had begun to encounter serious shortages of wood as far back as the days of Elizabethan England. Indeed, in terms of raw material inputs, the industrial revolution in the United Kingdom in the late eighteenth century and after may be characterized as a successful bypassing of constraints upon productive activity imposed by a severely limited wood supply. The early technological breakthroughs in fuel and power sources and metallurgy substituted coal and iron for the intensive reliance upon wood both as a fuel and as an industrial raw material.

In the United States the situation was vastly different. Whereas the early technological breakthroughs in the United Kingdom constituted an attempt at developing substitutes for scarce forest products, the United States possessed a rich abundance of such resources. In fact, much of what was unique in the American industrialization experience was attributable to the fact that the United States began her industrialization in a much more favorable resource position than western Europe generally. The innovative process in the United States in the early nineteenth century (and before) was a direct reflection of this circumstance. Whereas much of Britain's early industrialization effort should be understood as a deliberate attempt to overcome the constraints imposed by dependence upon organic materials, Americans possessed no similar inducement. In fact, a key to much of early American industrialization—certainly until at least the middle of the nineteenth century—should be understood in terms of a technology specifically geared to the intensive exploitation of natural resources which existed in considerable abundance relative to capital and labor. This background information is critical to the explanation of the fact that, in spite of America's late industrial start as compared to Britain, she quickly established a worldwide leadership in the design, production, and exploitation of woodworking machinery. By the middle of the nineteenth century a good deal of this initial advantage had already been dissipated. Subsequently the rising price of wood and the falling price of iron began to put the American economy back on a somewhat more conventional "European" track, and there occurred a shift from cordwood to coal in fuel, and from wood to iron as a raw material.[4]

The purely technical problems involved in the development of woodworking machinery should not be underestimated. There were many special problems involved that had no counterpart in metalworking. Richards has stated: "It is safe to assert that with their high speed and endless modification, wood machines demand a higher grade of ingenuity and skill in their construction than machines for cutting and shaping metal."[5] In contrast to metalworking machinery, woodworking machines were operated at very high rates of speed, and the nature of the materials upon which they worked was subject to a much wider degree of variability. "It is easy to calculate the strain and provide for the proper performance of cutting tools moving at sixteen feet a minute, but when these cutting edges are moved *five to ten thousand* feet in the same time, a new set of conditions are involved, conditions that cannot be predicated upon the ordinary laws of construction."[6]

The high speeds of woodworking machinery created unique problems with respect to the operation of shafts and cutters.

Special attention had to be paid to such matters as lubrication, balancing, centrifugal strain, bearings, etc. Whereas metalcutting machinery was designed to deal with metals which did not vary significantly in their physical characteristics and therefore their machining properties, woodworking machines had to deal with enormous variability. They worked materials ranging from soft fir-timbers, on the one hand, to woods of a hardness approaching cast iron—such as ebony—on the other. As a result, "Some of the leading manufacturers make as many as eighty different machines and modifications, which is the more surprising when we consider that they are all cutting machines, that is, working with sharp edges, and not to be contrasted with those for metal work, which include punching, forging and grinding machines."[7]

II

Victor Clark has pointed out that "The first patent issued in America for a mechanical invention was given, in 1646, by the colony of Massachusetts to Joseph Jenks, for improved sawmills and scythes."[8] This was a peculiarly appropriate prolog. Both inventions heralded—one in raw material processing and the other in agriculture—the development of a technology geared to the maximum utilization of natural resource inputs and the substitution, wherever possible, of abundant resources for scarce labor. Sawmills in colonial America, in fact, long antedated their introduction in England. Sawmills may possibly have been constructed by the Dutch on Manhattan Island as early as the 1620s, certainly by 1633. The first sawmill in England is reputed to have been built in 1663, but it was quickly destroyed and it was a century or so before sawmills began to be seriously used in England. Yet even as early as 1663 there were already hundreds of sawmills in New England. Their construction, often in conjunction with a gristmill, generally followed quickly upon the settlement of a new community.[9] The colonial emphasis upon the export of forest products is evident from the very beginning. The first ships returning from Jamestown carried "clapboards and wainscott," and the pilgrim settlers in Plymouth, after the harvest of 1621, collected lumber which they sent back to England.[10]

The abundance of wood in the American environment meant that the economic payoff to inventions which facilitated the exploitation of that abundant resource would also be likely to be very high. In particular, anything that reduced the price of inputs complementary to wood was especially welcome—e.g., nails. In fact, cost-reducing nailmaking machinery was one of the earliest classes of American inventions to excite the interest of Europeans. Apparently 23 patents for nailmaking machinery had been granted by the patent office before 1800. Perhaps the most notable figure in this development was Jacob Perkins of Newburyport, whose water-powered machinery for cutting and heading nails was patented on January 16, 1795. It ". . . was said to be capable of turning out 200,000 nails in a day."[11] The resulting reduction in the cost of cut nails in the first half of the nineteenth century was a significant contribution to the intensive utilization of wood for building purposes. The price of wrought nails, mostly imported, was about 25 cents a pound when the nailmaking machinery was first devised. The price declined to 8 cents a pound in 1828, to 5 cents by 1833, and to 3 cents a pound by 1842.[12] As a result, the cost of products made of wood was substantially reduced. This reduction in the relative cost of products fashioned out of wood in turn increased even further the large and rapidly growing market for woodworking machinery.[13]

Although no reliable basis for an accurate estimate is available, it is probable that most of the wood products fashioned by woodworking machinery consisted of building materials.[14] Indeed, the combination of cheap, machine-made nails, abundant wood supplies, and an expanding and improving armory of woodworking machines was directly responsible for a major American building innovation in the 1830s: the balloon frame house. The distinctive structural feature of the balloon frame house is that it systematically eliminated all the heavy members of the traditional New England frame house (or barn). It did away, furthermore, with the awkward and time-consuming mortising and tenoning method of joining. As Siegfried Giedion has put it: "The principle of the balloon frame involves the substitution of thin plates and studs—running the entire height of the building and held together only by nails—for the ancient and expensive method of construction with mortised and tenoned joints."[15] The critical importance of this technique is that its lightness and simplicity—the house was essentially nailed together with light 2-inch × 4-inch studs—sharply reduced the total labor requirements of construction and made it possible to substitute relatively unskilled labor for the skilled carpenter. What the invention lacked in elegance was more than compensated for by its highly utilitarian qualities and, above all, by its cheapness. Its characteristics were admirably suited to the American environment and its use spread rapidly across the country.[16]

It is, unfortunately, impossible to follow the growth in the number of sawmills in the United States with any pretensions of accuracy until the end of the period. It is not until the Census of 1840 that the data were tabulated with any sort of care.[17] The returns for 1840, 1850, and 1860 are presented in Tables 2, 3, and 4. It will be seen that the Census of 1840 reported 31,650 sawmills and a value of product of $12,943,507; for 1850 the number of sawmills was 17,475 and the value of product was $58,611,976; the Census of 1860 reported 20,658 sawmills and a value of product of $96,699,856. The apparent decline in the number of sawmill establishments between 1840 and 1850 may have been due to alterations in coverage. Defebaugh suggests that "It is probable that the 1840 report included independent shingle mills, cooperage shops, planing mills, etc., in the total . . ."[18]

Although Americans, as we have seen, applied power to the sawing of timber at a very early date, improvements in the saw itself came much later and more slowly. The simple up-and-down sash saw or frame saw, consisting ". . . of but a single blade surmounted in a frame of wood which surrounded the log,"[19] was the standard equipment from early colonial times

This vertical or sash saw was located in Chester Springs, Pennsylvania, and dates from the middle of the nineteenth century. In operation it made 100-130 strokes per minute while the log advanced 2 feet or more per minute. Courtesy: The National Museum of History and Technology, Smithsonian Institution.

until the middle of the nineteenth century. The sash saw began to give way to the gang saw and the muley saw in the 1840s. Although the muley saw was much faster than the old-fashioned sash saw, all these saws suffered from the functional limitations inherent in their intermittent, reciprocating action. It was therefore inevitable that they would eventually give way to the continuous cutting action of saws operated on different principles. Samuel Miller of Southampton, England, had patented the first circular saw in 1777, but it was not introduced into the United States until 1814.[20] Although its greater speed was an important advantage, it generated considerable heat at high velocities. "At high speeds the saw expanded and wobbled, and the sawyer found it difficult to follow true lines. Moreover, the saw could not cut logs larger than half of its diameter, and the size of the saw was limited. In order to cut large logs two or three saws were employed, one above the other."[21] The use of the circular saw therefore was for many years confined to specialized uses such as veneer cutting.[22]

All the saws mentioned so far possessed a common feature: they converted a distressingly large proportion of the timber into sawdust rather than lumber.

> The saws were thick and seven feet long, with large teeth, and would bear heavy feed. The boards sawed in the single mills looked rough, as the saws cut from one-half to three-quarter inches at the stroke, and made coarse sawdust. The gang saws had finer teeth, cut more slowly, and made finer sawdust, leaving the boards smooth even from knotty logs. Gang boards were sometimes used without planing. The quantity of sawdust shoved into the outlet from these mills in a year was enormous. The mill ponds below, the willow bars, eddies, etc., received these deposits; and the accumulation of years is still to be seen along the outlet, in bends and other places.[23]

The blade of the sash saws which still reigned supreme in the forests of Maine, New York, and Pennsylvania as late as 1840 was usually ⁵/₁₆ inch thick, and produced a kerf of over ⅜ inch. The later saws, whatever their other features, were no less wasteful of wood.

> Outside of the best gang mills, which form but a small share of the whole, it is safe to assume that one-fifth of all the timber sawed is converted into sawdust. Considering that the lumber of commerce in America consists mainly of one-inch boards, it might even be set down at one-fourth, after the stock is squared. Circular and muley saw mills made a kerf of about five-sixteenths of an inch wide, which, with the irregularity of the lines, may be counted as three-eighths of an inch, in the manufacture of a stock into one-inch boards, and gives us five-eighths lumber and three-eighths saw-dust.[24]

American circular saws used blades of thicker gauge than the English, and had their teeth spaced wide apart.[25] These were characteristics admirably suited for high speed of operation, but at the same time produced a very large kerf.

As lumber became increasingly expensive, toward the mid-nineteenth century (see Table 5), more and more inventive effort was directed toward reducing the waste.[26] The technical solution had been available, in principle, for some time, in the band saw. William Newberry of London had patented a band mill as early as 1808 and it seems to have been subsequently reinvented independently in the United States.[27] The band saw was basically a very simple invention. It consisted of an endless band of steel that passed over two wheels, giving the saw continuous rather than intermittent action. Not the least of its advantages was that it could cut logs of greater size than most circular saws. Its use, however, was held up until after the Civil War because of intractable technical problems. These included the difficulty in constructing a blade that would not snap when subjected to an unusual combination of torsional and other strains. In this respect, improvements in metallurgy eventually proved to be of vital importance.

The savings finally achieved by the adoption of the band saw were highly significant to an economy in which the price of lumber was rising.

The circular saw whose bits averaged five-sixteenths of an inch would turn 312 feet into sawdust for every thousand feet of inch boards. If the saw could be reduced to one-twelfth of an inch, which was the thickness of the early band saws, only 83 feet would be lost in sawdust.[28]

III

Planing machines were second only to saws in a ranking of woodworking machines by their relative importance, and they also typically followed the sawing operation in the processing of wood. In the first half of the nineteenth century a variety of planing machines were introduced, operating on different principles (carriage-planing machines, parallel-planing machines, and surface-planing machines[29]). The one that easily had the greatest impact, however, was the Woodworth planing machine, first patented by William Woodworth of Poughkeepsie, New York, on December 27, 1828. The invention represented a highly effective combination of feeding rolls and rotary cutting cylinders. Most references to the Woodworth planer are preoccupied with its tortuous history of litigation continuing into the 1850s, as the patent rights were extended and reissued. The patent did not finally expire until 1856. The many attempts to invent around this "notorious monopoly," as it was frequently called, led to numerous suits for patent infringement. This was hardly surprising, since planing was a critical woodworking operation and Woodworth's patent protection was defined so broadly that it was, indeed, most difficult to circumvent.

The planing machine had evolved, by 1850, into numerous specialized forms, each one well adapted to a particular product. The Woodworth machine was widely adopted for the manufacture of flooring boards, and variants of it were employed in boxmaking. Where an accurate, smooth surface was required, Daniel's traverse planing machine was far more satisfactory. "It consists of an upright frame, in which a vertical shaft revolves, having horizontal arms, at the ends of which are fixed the cutter. The work is carried along on a travelling bed under the cutters, which are driven at a very high speed."[30] Daniel's planing machine dominated in the heaviest classes of work on railroads and the manufacture of wagons, and where the nature of the timber presented special problems, as when it was twisted or warped.[31]

It is difficult in a short scope to follow woodworking invention through the subsequent stages of processing after sawing and planing, because from this point machinery design branched out in a multiplicity of directions to accommodate the highly specialized needs of a wide range of users. Mortising and tenoning machines were probably the most important subsequent categories, since this was the usual method of joining.[32] Mortising machines were much more complex than tenoning machinery, and were divided into reciprocating and rotary mortising machines. In America much greater reliance was placed upon the reciprocating machine than was the case elsewhere.[33]

Beyond this, however, there existed a wide array of specialized machinery for boring, slotting, dovetailing, edging, grooving, and so on. Further, within each of these categories of machines were modifications and alterations in design to meet the unique needs of particular classes of final products—shingles, laths, clapboards, staves, wagons, agricultural implements, boxes, stairs, sashes, doors, blinds, furniture, and veneers.

The parliamentary committee which visited the United States in 1854 was astonished at "the wonderful energy that characterizes the wood manufacture of the United States."[34] They were particularly impressed by precisely this extensive specialization of machinery. Whitworth states in his report:

The Daniel planer was used for heavy jobs such as railroad ties and in wagon manufacture. Courtesy: The National Museum of History and Technology, Smithsonian Institution.

Many works in various towns are occupied exclusively in making doors, window frames, or staircases by means of self-acting machinery, such as planing, tenoning, mortising, and jointing machines. They are able to supply builders with the various parts of the woodwork required in buildings at a much cheaper rate than they can produce them in their own workshops without the aid of such machinery. In one of these manufactories twenty men were making panelled doors at the rate of 100 per day.[35]

One special machine not so far mentioned deserves to be singled out, Thomas Blanchard's lathe for turning irregular forms. Blanchard's lathe was originally devised for the shaping of gunstocks. The gunstock had been the most serious bottleneck in the transition from the handicraft technology to the production of guns by machinery.[36] The highly irregular shape of the gunstock had long been an extremely tedious operation, since it involved separate hand activities of whittling, boring, and chiseling. Before Blanchard invented his first gunstocking machine in Millbury, Massachusetts, in 1818, a skilled man could produce only one or two gunstocks per day. Blanchard's lathe made it possible to reproduce any irregular shape by machinery by copying a model.

A pattern and block to be turned are fitted on a common shaft, that is so hung in a frame that it is adapted to vibrate toward or away from a second shaft that carries a guide wheel opposite and pressing against the pattern, and a revolving cutter wheel of the same diameter opposite the block to be turned. During the revolution of the pattern the block is brought near to or away from the cutting wheel, reproducing exactly the form of the pattern.[37]

Blanchard's lathe was an immediate success and it was introduced into the national armory at Springfield during the 1820s under Blanchard's personal supervision.[38] It quickly evolved

The Blanchard lathe, originally designed for production of gunstocks, could be used to produce any irregular shape. The original machine, shown here, is in the Springfield Armory. Courtesy: The National Museum of History and Technology, Smithsonian Institution.

from a single machine into a series of highly specialized machines. In fact,

> By 1827 Blanchard's stocking and turning machinery had been developed into 16 machines, in use at both national armories, and for the following purposes: sawing off stock, facing stock and sawing lengthwise, turning stock, boring for barrel, turning barrel, milling bed for barrel-breech and pin, cutting bed for tank of breech-plate, boring holes for breech-plate screws, gauging for barrel, cutting for plate, forming bed for interior of lock, boring side and tang-pin holes, and turning fluted oval on breech.[39]

Although Blanchard's lathe had been devised specifically for the production of gunstocks, it embodied a principle of far wider applicability in the development of automatic machinery. Indeed, it could be used to produce any irregular shape, and it was shortly introduced into making shoe lasts, hat blocks, spokes of wheels, and oars. But, in the longer run, it also provided vital design elements in the construction of specialized machinery for the manufacture of products of an interchangeable nature.

IV

This is not the appropriate place to speculate upon the reasons for the high aggregate level of inventive activity which Americans displayed in the first half of the nineteenth century.[40] But it does seem important to say something about the direction which such activity took, since that is a central concern of this essay.

Contemporaries as well as later writers have emphasized the laborsaving aspect of American technology, from the reports of the British parliamentary committees[41]—and others long before them—to Habakkuk's seminal work, *American and British Technology in the 19th Century* (Cambridge, 1962) which bears the subtitle, "The Search for Labour-saving Inventions."

What has been insufficiently stressed is that the technology both developed and adopted in the United States was a *resource-intensive* technology. The preoccupation with capital and labor in a two-factor view of the world has served to obscure the fundamental point that Americans pushed the technological frontier in directions where it was possible to substitute abundant natural resources *for either labor or capital*. Moreover, many of the American inventions which were so obviously laborsaving were also, necessarily and less obviously, resource-intensive in their operation.

In a highly resource-abundant environment such as the United States, it made excellent economic sense to trade off large doses of abundant raw material inputs for the scarcer factors of capital and labor. This was done in many ways. The "wastefulness" of wood which seemed to characterize American woodworking technology and to which Europeans so often called attention, was a general feature of America's technological adaptation.[42] Just as we developed and employed woodworking machinery which utilized wood more wastefully than did, say, European handicraft methods, so did we, at an early stage, build entire road surfaces out of wood, and construct large domestic fireplaces which were highly inefficient in fuel utilization but economized on the labor-intensive processes of chopping or sawing wood in order to accommodate smaller fireplaces or stoves (the stoves, of course, eventually came[43]). But, similarly, at an early stage we employed "inefficient" wooden pitchback waterwheels, which utilized only a small proportion of the waterpower available to them, since these wheels were very cheap to construct and therefore economized on scarcer capital. The same trade-off characterized our utilization of high-pressure steam engines aboard steamboats on western rivers. Such engines, as Louis Hunter has pointed out, were highly wasteful of fuel but considerably cheaper to construct than low-pressure engines. The latter were much more popular in the east where cordwood prices were considerably higher.[44] And finally, a major thrust of American agricultural invention in the nineteenth century was toward the development of a technology which maximized the acreage that could be cultivated by a single farmer. Here again is a substitution of an abundant input—agricultural land—for other scarcer factors of production. Doubtless a visitor from Japan or the Indian subcontinent would have been appalled at such "wastefulness," as were some observers of American woodworking technology.[45] The essential point, however, is that, when resource endowments differ significantly, one economy's "criminal wastefulness" may be another economy's optimal resource allocation.

All of this does, in fact, shed at least a glimmer of light upon the apparently high level of American inventive activity. The American economy entered into the process of industrialization at a point when her resource endowment—certainly in the cases of forest resources and agricultural land—was substantially more favorable than was the case in western Europe. This difference in endowment made it economically rational to search for inventions along portions of the invention possibility frontier which were not being carefully explored by Europeans on the grounds that they were inefficient. Thus, the Americans were the first people whose resources made it worthwhile to explore systematically the realm of highly resource-intensive inventions. And, as America's woodworking machinery abundantly demonstrated, there was a rich harvest of inventions available to an economy which could afford to trade off large quantities of natural resources for other factors of production.[46] This may also be an early evidence of American profligacy with our natural environment about which there is now so much intense concern.

Table 1.
Lumber Consumption for The United States and United Kingdom (specified years)

Year	United States		United Kingdom	
	Consumption in board feet (thousands)[1]	Per capita consumption	Consumption in board feet (thousands)[2]	Per capita consumption
1799	300,000	58	102,703	10
1809	400,000	57	121,916	10
1819	550,000	59	244,745	17
1829	850,000	67	319,306	20
1839	1,604,000	98	430,267[3]	23
1849	5,392,000	239	1,024,565[4]	50
1859	8,029,000	259	1,796,596	79
1869	12,755,543	328	2,419,390	95

[1]Henry B. Steer, *Lumber Production in the United States, 1799–1946* (Washington, D.C.: Government Printing Office, 1948), p. 10.

[2]U.K. figures: To 1839 "Accounts and Papers: Reports of the Commissioners, Estimates for the House of Commons," *Great Britain Customs and Excise Department Statistical Office: Annual Statement of Trade,* H.M.S.O.

[3]Figures to this year are only labeled as "Timber." This excludes Wooden Hoops, Deals, Battens, and Hardwoods imported for furniture. For an approximation of total consumption, add about 10 percent to all figures to 1839.

[4]U.K. figures after 1843 are from *Annual Abstracts of Statistics: Great Britain: 1840–1946* (London: Kraus-Thomson Ltd.), Kraus Reprint Nos. 1 to 84.

Table 2.

U.S. Census of 1840 Report on Sawmills

States and territories	Number of sawmills	Value of product in $	States and territories	Number of sawmills	Value of product in $
Alabama	524	169,008	Mississippi	309	192,794
Arkansas	88	176,617	Missouri	393	70,355
Connecticut	673	147,841	New Hampshire	959	433,217
Delaware	123	5,562	New Jersey	597	271,591
District of Columbia	1	......	New York	6,356	3,891,302
Florida	65	20,346	North Carolina	1,056	506,766
Georgia	677	114,050	Ohio	2,883	262,821
Illinois	785	203,666	Pennsylvania	5,389	1,150,220
Indiana	1,248	420,791	Rhode Island	123	44,455
Iowa	75	50,280	South Carolina	746	537,684
Kentucky	718	130,329	Tennessee	977	217,606
Louisiana	139	66,106	Vermont	1,081	346,939
Maine	1,381	1,808,683	Virginia	1,987	538,092
Maryland	430	226,977	Wisconsin	124	202,239
Massachusetts	1,252	344,845			
Michigan	491	392,325	Total—United States	31,650	$12,943,507

Table 3.
U.S. Census of 1850 Report on Sawmills

States and territories	Number of establishments	Capital in $	Number of wage-earners	Wages in $	Cost of raw material in $	Value of products in $
Alabama	173	952,473	937	164,268	529,976	1,103,481
Arkansas	66	113,575	275	42,828	31,719	122,918
California	10	147,200	114	175,080	38,050	959,485
Connecticut	239	308,150	371	97,392	277,831	534,794
Delaware	83	158,180	224	50,640	118,322	236,863
District of Columbia	1	5,000	14	2,400	22,500	29,000
Florida	49	271,400	499	99,072	121,216	391,034
Georgia	333	1,008,668	1,221	238,356	377,766	923,403
Illinois	468	843,535	1,306	298,524	591,508	1,324,484
Indiana	928	1,502,811	2,265	513,216	858,634	2,195,351
Iowa	144	204,475	344	81,348	225,135	470,760
Kentucky	466	1,029,980	1,490	306,324	721,889	1,592,434
Louisiana	138	892,785	948	226,452	273,694	1,129,677
Maine	732	3,009,240	4,439	1,301,376	3,609,247	5,872,573
Maryland	123	237,850	357	77,892	298,715	585,168
Massachusetts	448	1,369,275	1,337	396,576	834,847	1,552,265
Michigan	558	1,880,875	2,730	740,076	987,525	2,464,329
Minnesota	4	92,000	62	18,300	23,800	57,800
Mississippi	259	711,130	1,079	221,628	332,141	913,197

(see on for continuation)

Table 3.(continued)
U.S. Census of 1850 Report on Sawmills

States and territories	Number of establish- ments	Capital in $	Number of wage- earners	Wages in $	Cost of raw material	Value of products in $
Missouri	334	633,109	1,220	289,092	623,518	1,479,124
New Hampshire	545	859,305	969	265,068	622,564	1,099,492
New Jersey	324	928,500	665	177,180	646,209	1,123,052
New Mexico	1	5,000	4	864	10,000	20,000
New York	4,625	8,032,983	10,840	2,863,188	6,813,130	13,126,759
North Carolina	299	1,057,685	1,135	198,984	480,907	985,075
Ohio	1,639	2,600,361	3,756	924,084	1,693,688	3,864,452
Oregon	37	536,200	242	331,980	190,000	1,355,500
Pennsylvania	2,894	6,913,267	7,052	1,787,520	3,869,558	7,729,058
Rhode Island	51	138,700	134	60,252	142,768	241,556
South Carolina	353	1,106,033	1,431	203,220	525,844	1,108,880
Tennessee	451	707,280	1,229	192,612	283,607	725,387
Texas	89	300,075	426	96,912	156,148	466,012
Utah	5	12,400	18	....	....	14,620
Vermont	326	438,025	606	153,288	303,306	618,065
Virginia	2	17,000	10	2,460	419,536	977,412
Wisconsin	278	1,006,892	1,569	419,340	538,237	1,218,516
Total—United States	17,475	$40,031,417	51,218	$13,017,792	$27,593,535	$58,611,976

Table 4.
U.S. Census of 1860 Report on Sawmills

States and territories	Number of establish-ments	Capital in $	Number of wage-earners	Wages in $	Cost of materials used in $	Value of products in $
Alabama	339	1,756,947	1,686	428,268	692,027	1,875,628
Arkansas	178	583,690	969	268,716	303,137	1,158,902
California	295	1,948,327	1,924	1,474,626	1,215,244	4,003,431
Connecticut	208	386,800	311	89,878	377,580	589,456
Delaware	71	247,760	176	48,132	154,500	276,161
District of Columbia	1	20,000	4	1,680	17,000	21,125
Florida	87	1,282,000	1,222	316,292	541,531	1,476,645
Georgia	411	1,639,717	1,872	438,828	1,211,807	2,414,896
Illinois	463	1,446,088	1,798	497,280	1,153,237	2,681,295
Indiana	1,331	2,544,538	3,631	1,001,034	1,734,483	4,451,114
Iowa	561	1,656,535	1,762	478,080	1,071,285	2,185,206
Kansas	124	395,940	497	204,920	538,882	1,563,487
Kentucky	482	1,405,835	1,665	439,080	990,021	2,495,820
Louisiana	161	1,213,726	1,039	286,956	548,647	1,575,995
Maine	926	4,401,482	4,969	1,453,739	4,504,368	7,167,762
Maryland	187	472,800	377	101,208	239,808	609,044
Massachusetts	611	1,419,473	1,408	421,548	1,570,362	2,353,153
Michigan	986	7,735,780	6,980	1,895,162	3,425,613	7,303,404
Minnesota	163	1,349,620	1,175	371,988	603,095	1,257,603
Mississippi	229	1,049,910	1,441	436,116	653,157	1,832,227

(see on for continuation)

Table 4. (continued)

U.S. Census of 1860 Report on Sawmills

States and territories	Number of establish- ments	Capital in $	Number of wage- earners	Wages in $	Cost of materials used in $	Value of products in $
Missouri	548	1,809,725	1,753	477,372	1,398,564	3,085,026
Nebraska	46	127,800	155	43,648	113,750	335,340
New Hampshire	567	1,185,126	1,195	341,160	702,111	1,293,706
New Jersey	268	1,163,100	591	188,752	942,706	1,623,160
New Mexico	9	45,100	42	14,520	12,950	45,150
New York	3,035	7,931,708	8,798	2,369,720	5,531,704	10,597,595
North Carolina	349	941,880	1,354	296,952	510,379	1,176,013
Ohio	1,911	3,708,153	4,327	1,209,386	2,521,481	5,279,883
Oregon	126	⸙ 430,400	378	210,312	189,925	690,008
Pennsylvania	3,078	10,978,464	9,419	2,485,103	5,211,990	10,994,060
Rhode Island	26	66,000	79	21,828	46,027	76,114
South Carolina	361	1,145,116	1,263	219,361	498,290	1,125,640
Tennessee	546	1,492,013	1,867	435,536	880,595	2,228,503
Texas	194	1,278,080	1,211	365,376	530,545	1,754,206
Utah	28	151,656	67	46,460	61,973	145,505
Vermont	415	862,060	939	244,551	477,798	928,541
Virginia	784	1,292,886	2,139	464,182	911,714	2,218,962
Washington	33	1,168,000	653	383,130	424,671	1,194,360
Wisconsin	520	5,785,355	4,703	1,227,385	2,067,816	4,616,430
Total—United States	20,658	$74,519,590	75,852	$21,698,365	$44,580,773	$96,099,856

Table 5.

Wholesale Price Index of U.S. Lumber, 1798–1869
(1910–14 = 100)

Year	Index	Year	Index
1798	24	1834	31
1799	23	1835	31
1800	24	1836	32
1801	27	1837	45
1802	27	1838	45
1803	24	1839	45
1804	26	1840	42
1805	27	1841	43
1806	27	1842	40
1807	27	1843	37
1808	26	1844	39
1809	26	1845	43
1810	26	1846	42
1811	25	1847	41
1812	24	1848	41
1813	25	1849	40
1814	27	1850	43
1815	37	1851	43
1816	35	1852	46
1817	31	1853	47
1818	28	1854	48
1819	28	1855	51
1820	27	1856	52
1821	26	1857	53
1822	25	1858	48
1823	26	1859	46
1824	26	1860	46
1825	27	1861	45
1826	28	1862	48
1827	29	1863	58
1828	29	1864	74
1829	28	1865	79
1830	27	1866	87
1831	29	1867	83
1832	29	1868	80
1833	30	1869	75

Source: *Historical Statistics of the United States: Colonial Times to 1957*
(Washington, D.C.: Government Printing Office, 1960), p. 317.

Early Lumbering: A Pictorial Essay

Charles E. Peterson

Two AND a half centuries lay between the founding of Virginia, when the forests of the James River were first put to the ax, and the visit of English experts to the New York Industrial Exhibition of 1854. In that interval woodworking techniques had become highly developed in this country, and the visitors were amazed to learn that one man in a steampowered factory could make five panelled doors in a day.[1]

While today we regret the decimation of our virgin forests, our forefathers had different priorities. Cleared forests fulfilled two urgent needs: cropland and cheap lumber. American lumber was also used to build the colonial West Indies, and axmen from Hawaii worked the Oregon forests to build Honolulu. According to the census of 1860 the lumber industry —with a product valued at $99 million—had become the second largest in the United States.

Relatively little has been written about the lumber business; the men who built it—like constructors generally—were not literary types. From the evolution of the American felling ax and the camp songs of lumberjacks, to the mass production of jigsaw cornices and California Gold Rush prefabs, an immense range of subjects remains to be studied.[2] Despite the dearth of written materials, much can be learned from pictures.

EUROPEAN PRECEDENT

"The invention that moulded the character of American architecture was the sawmill," a team of authors remarked some years ago.[3] Surprisingly, the first sawmills of the New World trace their origin directly to continental Europe rather than to Britain. Samuel Smiles, the English biographer, noted that "the first sawmill in England was erected by a Dutchman near London in 1663 but was shortly abandoned in consequence of the determined hostility of the workmen." The next attempt a century later was also pulled down by a mob.[4] Documentary evidence clearly reveals that it was the expertise of Continental mechanics that made sawmills possible in the colonies.

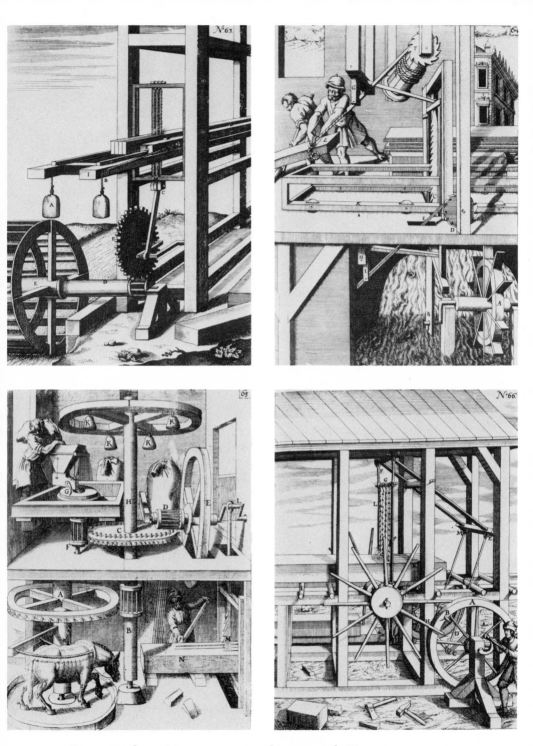

Saws, singly or in gangs, variously powered. From
Georgium Andream Bocklerum, *Theatrum Machinarum
Novvum*, Noribergae, 1662. Courtesy: American
Philosophical Society.

THE DUTCH IN THE NEW WORLD

Mechanical sawing first appeared in the Virginia colony on the James River as early as the summer of 1611. Technicians had been recruited at Hamburg "to build Saw mills & Seat them at ye falls." This made possible the new town of Henrico which had three streets of well-framed houses before it was burned by Indians in 1622.[5]

There are many seventeenth-century records of Dutch mills on the Hudson. One of the first was a windmill built on Nutten Island (modern Governor's Island) in New York Harbor as early as 1623.[6] Its lease by the West India Company in 1639 recorded twenty saws and a variety of other equipment on the premises.

As early as 1630 Dutch sawyers were sent direct from Holland to Fort Orange (modern Albany), and the industry rapidly spread along the Upper Hudson. The Earl of Bellomont reported to the Lords of Trade in London in 1701 that Henry Livingston had a Dutch millwright put up an apparatus with twelve saws and that the forty sawmills in the province were destroying "more timber than all the sawmills in New Hampshire."[7]

In 1714 crates of Dutch saws were sent via Nantes to the new French colony of Louisiana[8] and two Dutch carpenters were sent along to set them up. It was intended to open a commerce in lumber with the French and Spanish colonies in the West Indies as well as supply the home ports.

Old sawmill (*zaagmolen*) at Zaandam, Holland. From G. Husslage, *Windmolens*, Amsterdam, 1968.

BRINGING IN THE LOGS

The ax and the saw were among the earliest tools invented by man, and in the earliest times lumber was sawed right where the trees fell. In this country two-man saws—operated over pits or on platforms—produced the first boards. But mills could do the work of twenty or more hand sawyers. It then became necessary to haul the logs to the mill on wagons by horses or oxen or to drag them over frozen ground in winter.

Water transport was introduced early on the tidal James River. The Eastern climax in rafting was seen on the Hudson, Delaware, and Susquehanna rivers only in the 1850s when great rafts descending the rivers became a familiar sight. Those shown in the view opposite are probably of white pine from the newly opened Chippewa lands in Wisconsin. On the Ohio and Mississippi Rivers rafts sometimes floated a thousand miles, carrying prospective settlers with them. The making of logs and their assembly and navigation in rafts required special gear and considerable skill.

Canals also served to transport lumber. The timber from New Hampshire bound for the coast had been often damaged in shooting the falls of the Merrimack but the Middlesex Canal, after completion in 1803, provided a safer route.[9] Regulations show that rafts 9½ x 75 feet could be joined into trains 500 feet long and drawn by horses or oxen at the rate of one and a half miles per hour.[10] They were received and temporarily stored behind the big boom at the Charlestown "Pond," to be used in the fast-growing city of Boston or traded in distant ports.

In the nineteenth century the lumbermills of the great river towns like Cincinnati, St. Louis, and New Orleans were fed from such rafts. Their woodworking plants equipped with new types of machinery could supply the whole West.

"Drawing the Logs to the Creek, [as done in] Maine and New Brunswick," *Harper's Weekly*, 1858.
Courtesy: Virginia Daiker and the Library of Congress.

"Rafts at the Mouth of the St. Croix, Wisconsin." From Henry Lewis, *The Valley of the Mississsippi Illustrated*, St. Paul, 1967 (first edition 1854).

SPOFFORD-MORSE SAWMILL

In November 1925 the Spofford-Morse sawmill at Uptack Hill near the village of Georgetown, Massachusetts, was disassembled and moved to Greenfield Village in Michigan, where it was re-erected and placed on public view. Said to have been built in 1682 and the oldest in the United States, it was described at the time of moving by W. W. Taylor:[11]

This picture shows some of the parts taken from the old mill.

In the fore-ground is the "Nigger-wheel" and wooden shaft, which shows the wooden cogs cut into the shaft itself. Just why the 2nd set was cut I can not understand, unless the first set wore out, and the shaft was then set over a little and the new set was then cut.

The Nigger-wheel at the right shows the oak pins whereby the carriage could be run back by foot power, which was probably the first method of backing up the carriage. The Water power "flutter-wheel" may have been installed later(?). This would have given the mill much more speed as it was a slow job to "kick it back" with the foot, and by jumping up and down on the pins to do this. I have seen it done many times and thus know what I am writing about.

Just in front of the Nigger-wheel can be seen the "Headblock" and at the right can be seen (imperfectly) the cast iron scroll wheel (or rather one of them, for there were two, both set on a large wooden shaft, on the inner end of which was the crank-wheel. These wheels were sometimes called "Rose wheels" as the water would fly out at each side like the blossom of a rose, when running under a "full head" of water. The tail race of the mill runs just in front of the mill, and is the whole brook.

Looking through the mill one can see one of the log runs whereon the logs were rolled into the mill. I saw no signs of a chain-haul from the pond, and doubt if there ever was one not-with-standing the miss-leading reports in the Haverhill news papers.

Spofford-Morse mill before moving. Courtesy: Henry Ford Museum, Dearborn, Michigan.

"THE COMPLEATEST SAW-MILL IN AMERICA"

Thomas Anburey was an officer of General Burgoyne's Army on its ill-fated expedition to Albany in the summer of 1777. Writing to a friend on July 5 he enclosed "a few drawings . . . [including] a representation of the block-house and saw mill, as being a very romantic view."[12] It appeared later on this copperplate as "A View of a Saw Mill & Block House upon Fort Anne Creek the property of Gen. Skeene which on Gen. Burgoyne's Army advancing was set Fire to by the Americans." Fort Anne is now landmarked by a village of that name; the cascade above it is known as Kane's Falls.

In 1758 Captain Phillip Skene, a Scot, had come up to Lake Champlain with the 27th Enniskillen Regiment of Foot in an operation against the French at Fort Ticonderoga. Impressed by the opportunities for development he petitioned for land and received a royal patent of some 29,000 acres at the very foot of the lake. Skenesborough (now Whitehall, New York) lay at the base of what is still known as Skene Mountain. The chief product of this enterprise was to have been lumber for the St. Lawrence market.

Skene called his burned mill "the compleatest saw-mill in America" and in seeking reparations, declared that he set fire to it himself. In any case, after Burgoyne's surrender at Saratoga he was marched off to New England as a prisoner of war.[13]

Sawmill near Fort Anne, New York, copperplate from sketch of 1777. Courtesy: Library of Congress.

OLIVER EVANS' SAWMILL, 1795

Oliver Evans of Philadephia (1755–1819) was the outstanding American figure in the early development of milling machinery and high-pressure steam engines. *The Young Mill-Wrights' & Millers' Guide*,[14] is mostly about gristmilling, but Evans included this well-known plate (No. XI) to delineate a water-power sawmill. It has been called "probably the first example of the American engravers' art to portray a piece of machinery for a technical work." The mill shown is 52 feet × 12 feet in size and is powered by a "flutter-wheel" (no. 11). Evans wrote:[15]

Of Saw-Mills—Their Utility

THEY are for sawing timber into all kinds of scantling, boards, lathes, &c. &c. are used to great advantage where labour is dear. One mill, attended by one man, if in good order, will saw more than 20 men with whip-saws, and much more exactly.

Construction of their Water-wheels

They have been variously constructed; the most simple and useful of which, where water is plenty, and above six feet fall, is the flutter-wheel; but where water is scarce, in some cases, and for want of sufficient head in others, to give flutter-wheels sufficient motion, high wheels, double geared, have been found necessary.

Flutter-wheels may be made suitable for any head above six feet, by making them low and wide for low heads and high and narrow for high ones, so as to make about 120 revolutions or strokes of the saw, in a minute: but rather than double gear I would be satisfied with

. . . The Mechanism of a complete saw-mill is such as to produce the following effects, viz.

1. To move the saw up and down, with a sufficient motion and power.

2. To move the log to meet the saw with an uniform motion.

3. To stop of itself when within 3 inches of being through the log.

4. To draw the carriage with the log back by the power of water ready to enter again.

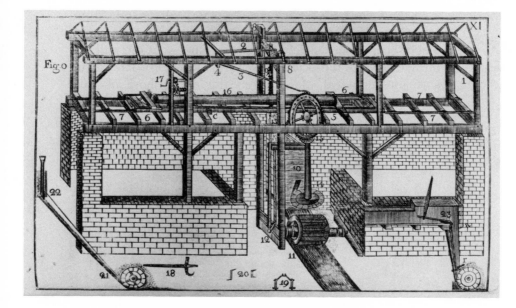

Oliver Evans' sawmill, 1795, engraving by J. Yeager.
Courtesy: Library Company of Philadelphia.

STEAM-POWERED MILLS

The American Citizen and General Advertiser of New York City for March 17, 1802, gives notice of a steam sawmill erected by the enterprising Robert M'Keen of Philadelphia. The earliest such mill we have discovered, it was located on a Delaware River wharf at Bordentown. Its proprietor offered cash for sawlogs of all descriptions, mahogany excepted. The advantage of being able to move such a mill *to the timber* was predicted. M'Keen also noted that the mill refuse could be used for fuel and wood ashes were excellent for fertilizer. The familiar hazards to the waterpower mill of draught and flood would also be eliminated.[16]

A few weeks later a sawmill burning coal was "the wonder of New York. People are continually running to look at it being something new . . . [it] will soon make a fortune for the owner" was the report.[17]

In the following year, when a New Orleans steamboat ran ashore, one William Donaldson used its engine to saw 3,000 feet of boards per day and made a fortune—but the mill was burned down by the local hand sawyers. Donaldson later set up a steam engine at Manchac on the north shore of Lake Maurepas with a pair of millstones and four saws.[18] Stationary steam engines soon spread up the Mississippi River and down the Ohio. By the year 1860, 174 of Ohio's 437 sawmills were powered by steam, and makers of the newly popular *circular* saws were advertising widely.

Raltson steam-powered mills, broadside. Courtesy: Donald Hutzlar and the Ohio Historical Society.

PATENT PORTABLE
SAW-MILL!

ANDREW RALSTON

Of Washington County and State of Pennsylvania, has obtained Letters Patent of the United States for improvements in Portable Saw-mills, and as he has tested the utility of said improvements by putting several mills into operation, both by horse and steam power, he now invites the attention of all persons interested in Saw-mills, Lumber, &c., particularly Ship-builders, Car-builders, and all others using long lumber, to examine said Mills, as lumber of any length can be

CUT PERFECTLY TRUE!

As there is no chance of the log springing.

The Saw and Pitman runs horizontal, cutting the top of the log, has teeth on both edges, cutting both ways and leaving no stump shot, is much easier attended and kept in order, and less liable to get out of order, can be moved at small expense from one neighborhood to another, requires less power to operate and costs less money than any other construction of Mill that will do the same amount of work. The subscriber has a short time since put one of said mills in operation at Mr. Hugh Graham's farm, 8 miles South West of Columbus, Ohio, and will remain there for a short time, and wishes persons to call and examine it as he will dispose of rights on reasonable terms. Come and examine the mill, as you may benefit the public, and make some money by so doing. I have arrangements with Messrs. McGilvray & Bell, of Sharon, Mercer County, Pennsylvania, to build any number of mills that may be wanted on moderate terms. They are energetic mechanics and will do their work well.

Any person wishing any information in relation to these Mills, or Rights, can get it by addressing the subscriber, West Middletown, Washington County, Pennsylvania.

ANDREW RALSTON.

The undersigned having helped to set up and put in operation one of Ralston's Patent Portable Saw-mills, and run it, we are fully satisfied of its utility, being easy to attend, using less power and doing more work with one saw and the same power, than any other Mill. We have no hesitation in recommending sa'd Mills to the attention of the public, and to Saw-mill and Lumber men in particular.

JAMES McBRIDE,
Millwright, Allegheny County, Pennsylvania.
E. M. WOODBURY,
HUGH GRAHAM,
Proprietor of said Mill.
March 19, 1855.
DAVID FINLEY.

SPECIAL DEVICES—SAWING SHINGLES

Shingles—small, thin, tapered boards used for covering roofs—have been around for a long time; the word comes from the Latin *scindula*. Europeans used them as long as wood was plentiful, and they were employed almost universally in America until very recent times.

The earliest method of making shingles was by splitting from "bolts" of log using an iron blade or "frow" struck with a wooden mallet. A fine shingle was made with straight grained wood—red and white cedar when available were generally preferred. Standard lengths were 18, 24, and 36 inches. Before being nailed in place, shingles were normally smoothed or "dressed" by hand using a draw knife.

When the steam engine and the circular saw became available, the sawn shingle came into its own. Less durable than the split article, it was much cheaper. In the year 1858 alone the United States Patent Office issued twenty patents for shingle machines and their parts.

Sawing shingles from the bolt. For public demonstration, this saw, patented by Robert Law of Portage City, Wisconsin in 1858, is cutting shingles by horsepower. Courtesy: W. J. Patterson and Upper Canada Village.

HORSE-POWERED MILLS

Horse-powered mills were in use from the eighteenth century in many places. The one illustrated may be viewed seasonally at Upper Canada Village. The saw assembly was one patented (#19,033) by Robert Law of Portage City, Wisconsin, in 1858.[19]

The great proliferation of American woodworking machines for sawing, planing, sanding, grooving, mortising and tenoning, etc.,—patented and otherwise—present a still unanswered challenge to the historians of building technology.

Four-horse mill at Upper Canada Village, Ontario. Animals were often used on the frontier when waterpower was unavailable. Here the operator with a whip could stand on the little platform in the middle making sure that all four animals were pulling their load.

PHILADELPHIA SAWS

Almost from its beginnings Philadelphia was noted for the number and diversity of its manufactures. Edwin W. Freedley in his *Hand-book* for 1857, extolling Philadelphia's industrial virtues, lists nine separate establishments making saws. Of two leading firms he wrote:

> The works now known as Rowland's Saw Works were founded by William Rowland in 1802, and are believed to be the oldest established of the kind in this country. They have supplied, and continue to supply, a large proportion of the large-sized Saws in use, Mill and Cross-cut, varying in length from six to eighteen feet. About fifty hands are engaged in this establishment, and two hundred Saws are produced daily. . . .

> The "Keystone Works," of which Mr. Henry Disston is proprietor, are probably the largest of the kind in the country. They consist of four buildings—three of them three stories high, and cover an area of over 20,000 square feet. The Machinery is of the most complete description, and driven by an engine of seventy-horse power. The Saws made at this establishment comprise nearly every variety, though principally Cast-steel Circular, Hand, and Panel Saws, all of which are tempered by *Sylvester's Patent Tempering Machine*, and the Circular Saws are ground by Southwell's Patent Grinding Machine. Among the novelties produced in this establishment might be mentioned, the *Patent Combination Saw*, comprising a perfect twenty-four inch square, straight edge, twenty-four inch rule and scratch-awl, and a handsaw, with a patent attachment for gauging any required depth.

> Mr. Disston employs one hundred and fifty hands. . . .

HENRY DISSTON,

Manufacturer of the Celebrated Cast-Steel, Patent, Ground Mill, Cross-cut and Circular Saws; also, the Patent Combination Saw, which comprises a 24-inch Square, Rule, and Plumb, a Scratch-Awl and Saw: it is one of the most useful tools a mechanic can have. Also, Hand, Panel, Ripping, Tenon, Wood, Web, Veneer, and Segment Saws; also, Trowels, Butchers' Saws, Saw and Straw Knives, Squares, Bevels, Gauges, and Slaw-Cutters, Trunk Springs, &c. &c. Saw Mandrels, of the most approved styles, always on hand.

MANUFACTORY, LAUREL ST., BELOW FOURTH,
Philadelphia.

Illustration from *McElroy's Philadelphia City Directory for 1860*. Courtesy: Historical Society of Pennsylvania.

Blandy's portable steam engine and saw mills, lithograph,
A. Hoen & Company. Courtesy: Library of Congress.

Artisans in Wood:
The Mathematical Instrument-Makers

Silvio A. Bedini

THE PREOCCUPATION of early American craftsmen with the use of wood has been well documented by American historians. The trades and crafts which customarily used wood as their primary working material, ranging from the housewright, carpenter, and joiner to the wheelwright, cooper, clockmaker and even the ship's carver have all been the subjects of published study. One craft that utilized wood for its products has, however, been overlooked thus far—the maker of mathematical instruments who was forced by the limited availability of metal to turn to wood for the tools to serve the early American men of science.

In fact, the early American men of science have themselves escaped the historian's attention. These were the mathematical practitioners, a countless number of more or less anonymous colonists self-taught in and linked together by the practical sciences required for colonization, settlement, and expansion. Rarely were the individual accomplishments of these "little men of science" of sufficient importance to achieve acknowledgment, but their combined efforts and pervasive influence on the practical sciences throughout the British colonies in North America combined literally to forge and shape the new nation. Their numbers included the cartographers who explored and mapped the wilderness, and the navigators who established trade along the coastal and inland waters and eventually across the sea routes to the rest of the world. There were also the surveyors who defined the bounds of personal property as well the boundaries of the colonies, territories, and future states, and the science teachers who trained more men to undertake these tasks by teaching courses in surveying and navigating in evening schools. Finally, there were also the philomaths—the occasional amateurs of science who made astronomical observations, calculated ephemerides for almanacs, and formed the first collections of natural and artificial curiosities which became the earliest science-museum collections in America. Linking all the others were the makers of mathematical instruments, the tools with which these practitioners accomplished their work. These were the most sophisticated products of the trades, arts, and crafts of colonial America, produced by skilled artisans in New England and the Middle Colonies who worked in both brass and wood.

Many of the instruments were simple works, their design basic to their purpose, with elemental construction and no elaboration. But each of them required graduated scales of reasonable accuracy, for they were all used for some type of measurement. Whereas it was a relatively simple matter for a skilled worker to produce the wooden or metallic elements of the instrument, the precise graduation and inscription of the scale upon these materials was a more complicated matter. It was a task for an engraver, and during the early period there were few if any skilled engravers in America, with tools and techniques that were rudimentary at best.

The first instruments produced in the New World were those required by the shipmaster and ship's officers. For the most part, these were traditionally made of wood with occasional small brass fittings; consequently, the skills of the colonial woodworker were the first to be applied to the new trade of the instrument-maker. The most common navigational instruments were the marine compass, the traverse board, the cross-staff, the backstaff, the octant, and the nocturnal.

The marine compass consisted generally of a compass fly, composed of a wind rose engraved on paper, to the back of which a magnetized iron wire was attached by means of glued strips. This fly was supported upon a brass pivot inside a turned

Eighteenth-century American dry-card compass with turned
wooden bowl, brass cover and crude gimbal suspension.
Courtesy: New London County Historical Society.

circular wooden case, the opening of which was protected by a pane of glass sealed in putty. Gimbals were later added to the brass or wooden bowl so that the compass remained always horizontal to the plane of the ship. Except for the engraved card, little skill was required to construct the marine compass, and it remained unchanged for centuries. Modified versions were introduced from time to time, but in general the most complicated feature was the graduated compass card produced by an engraver.

Somewhat more complicated was the cross-staff and its successor, the backstaff or Davis improved quadrant. The major components of these instruments were one or more extended limbs made of well-seasoned straight-grained hardwood. The selection of the pieces of wood required experience, and the success of the completed instrument depended greatly on the characteristics of the pieces chosen.

The cross-staff consisted of a wooden rule 36 inches long, having graduated scales engraved upon its four sides. One, two, or three transversals, or slabs of wood having a square opening through the center, were fitted to the staff and slid back and forth along its length. Again, the greatest skill needed was in the engraving of the scales. The cross-staff was replaced first by the backstaff and later by an improved version known as the Davis improved quadrant, which became the most important of the instruments in use in American waters prior to the middle of the eighteenth century. It consisted of a simple framework having two curved arcs engraved with scales. Three wooden blocks called vanes were attached at various points to enable the navigator to sight the sun. The inherent simplicity of the backstaff prohibited any great degree of modification and it remained unchanged throughout almost two centuries. Once again, the major skill required was in the division and engraving of the scales on the two wooden arcs. The nocturnal, which enabled the navigator to determine time at night, was another simple device, made entirely of wood, formed from two disks, engraved with scales and having index arms. The traverse board, another of the navigator's instruments, was likewise made entirely of wood, but because it did not require engraved scales, it was much simpler to produce.[1]

The first examples of these instruments in the New World were brought on the first voyages from England. The few that existed in the early settlements were greatly prized, because it was extremely difficult and expensive to import others, to say nothing of the long delay caused by the sea voyage from England. For all these reasons the colonists sought means to produce their own instruments as soon as possible.

Three basic problems faced them, however. First, the instruments used on shipboard required wood that was impervious to the moisture and salt of the sea air. Attempts to utilize native hardwoods were generally unsuccessful because they were softer than tropical woods, and more easily affected by the weather. Tropical woods were essential, but they had to be imported from England in small quantities and at a great price. The preferred woods were lignum vitae, mahogany, rosewood, and ebony, closely grained woods with an oil content that made them resistant to moisture. Boxwood and pearwood were particularly desirable for the parts requiring inscription of scales, because they were close-grained and light-textured without visible striation. Occasionally pearwood in sufficient size could be found locally. Rock maple, wild black cherry, and apple served as substitutes. For instance, the earliest known surviving scientific instrument made in America is a backstaff produced by James Halsey of Salem in 1676, constructed entirely of pearwood obtained locally from a single tree.[2]

By the early eighteenth century small quantities of tropical woods became available in major port cities, some brought in trade with England and the West Indies, and other supplies acquired from privateering ventures. It was not until midcentury, however, that tropical woods were imported in substantial quantities. Shipments of such woods were advertised in the local press from time to time. In August 1737, for example, the Boston newspapers announced the sale "on the Long Wharffe of Lignumvitae, Box wood, Ebony, Mahogany Plank, Sweet Wood Bark, and Wild Cinnamon Bark," while in November of

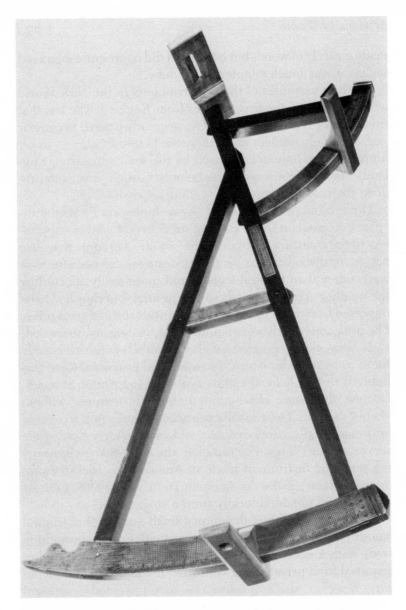

American backstaff of lignum vitae with boxwood scales
made by Joseph Holbeche in 1738 for Captain Joseph
Swan. Courtesy: National Museum of History and
Technology, Smithsonian Institution.

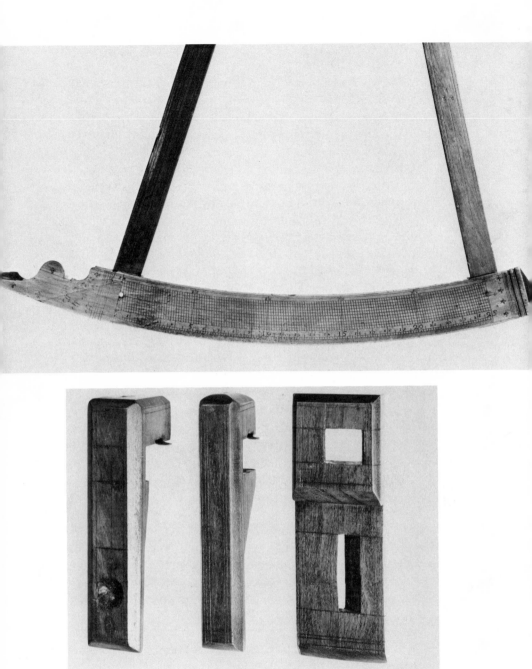

Details of engraved scale and vanes of Holbeche backstaff.

the same year a public sale was announced at the Exchange Tavern of "50 pieces of fine Mahogany in 10 Lots." Still another announcement in the Boston press a few years later noted the arrival of a shipment of "a parcel of Lignum vitae and 3½ inch Mahogany."[3]

At the same time wood-importing became a new profession. Among the first importers of record was John Waghorne of Boston, who advertised in 1740 that he could supply the best of "Turnery ware of Mahogany, etc."[4] The tropical woods supplied by occasional imports were supplemented more and more as time went on with stocks of mahogany and lignum vitae forming part of the cargoes of prize ships taken from the French and Spanish and brought into New England ports, and then advertised for public sale. After the middle of the eighteenth century the continuing supply of tropical hardwoods became adequate for the furniture-maker and for the instrument-maker as well. The surviving records of instrument-makers late in the century list an impressive variety of such materials, most of them woods obtained from the West Indies.

An invaluable and virtually unique source of information is the account books of Clark Elliott of New London, Conn., a maker of navigational instruments, maintained from 1767 until his death in 1793. In this record Elliott listed each of the 403 quadrants or backstaves he produced during his career. Of the total, 158 of his backstaves were made of green ebony, 62 of iron wood, and others of black ebony, marble wood, and speckled wood, in that order. He used also red wood, naked wood, cocas, plane, red stopper, bastard cocas, pearwood, brazeletomet, boxwood, lingoram, shittim wood, and even thorn wood. Frequently he combined two woods in the same instruments, such as cocas and plane, or green ebony and cocas.[5]

Many of the names of these woods as rendered by Elliott are unfamiliar today, and there is doubt concerning the actual identity of some of the woods listed. The green ebony used by the colonial maker was probably not true green ebony (*Diospyros melanoxylon*), but more probably the West Indian grandilla tree (*Vrya ebeneus*), which was also the source of cocas wood. These were generally imported from Jamaica and elsewhere in the West Indies. Black ebony was available from a variety of sources, but only the lesser qualities were used for instruments because of the cost of the best strains and their desirability for fine furniture. For example, African ebony, which was shipped from the Cape of Good Hope in relatively small billets, was considered inferior in color and grain to the ebony obtained from Mauritius or East Indies. It was therefore more readily available to English makers of mathematical and philosophical instruments.

Ironwood was in actuality not a single wood but the name given to a number of woods of various species derived from several parts of the tropical world. Ironwood used in the American colonies was probably imported from the West Indies. One variety referred to as ironwood in this period and also known as Red Stopper was obtained from the same region. Marblewood was generally found in Ceylon. Brazeletomet was exported from Brazil to Europe by Portuguese and Spanish traders, and was known by various other names, including brazilwood.[6]

Naturally, the earliest makers of scientific instruments in the colonies specialized first in the production of those required for navigation. Not only were these the instruments for which there was the greatest need, but they could be more readily produced than brass instruments. Skill was soon developed in copying English prototypes, and in their repair. Pieces of seasoned tropical woods were selected and shaped with tools of the cabinetmaker in the required standard sizes and forms. The backstaff, for example, was assembled with mortise-and-tenon joints and pinned together with fine brass nails, produced by the techniques of the pinmaker. Brass wire was formed by pulling it through iron plates by means of hand or waterpower until the appropriate dimension was achieved, and the wire then cut into the required lengths, and finished by one of several means.

The most difficult step was the engraving of the scales. A

metal scale of equal parts was used to lay out the divisions, which were then marked and numbered by incising evenly spaced lines in the wood, and the graduations were then lettered and numbered by stamping the wood with small iron dies. These sets of tiny die stamps were at first imported from England, but later colonial capability permitted their production in the New World. They remained standard throughout the period, so much so that it is almost impossible to distinguish between unsigned English and American instruments.

Because the navigational instruments were tools of measure made of wood, it was essential that there be no warping. It is a credit to the instrument-makers of old that the combination of selected seasoned woods and the assembling technique were such that even after hundreds of years surviving instruments in most instances retain their accuracy.

This problem of warping became even greater with the invention of the octant, an instrument of much greater precision, likewise made entirely of wood at first except for minor parts of brass or mirror. The first octants were large, shaped and fashioned after the style of the predecessor backstaff. Mahogany and rosewood were favored woods for early examples because they appeared to be less liable to warping, although it was later discovered that warpage nevertheless occurred. One solution was to reduce the overall size of the instrument, not only to prevent warping, but to lessen the weight and size, rendering it more convenient for use on the deck of a rolling ship. In reduced size, the octant could be made of ebony, which proved even stronger than mahogany and rosewood; thereafter, it was traditionally made of this wood. The warping that did occur in these instruments was rarely readily visible but was sufficient to make the octant inaccurate. With the advent of the sextant, an instrument of the same type derived from the same scientific principle, the problem was reduced by producing the latter almost always in cast brass and in a considerably smaller size.

As the maker of wooden navigational instruments flourished in port cities and shipping communities, other uses were found

Early American octant, maker not known, late eighteenth century. The instrument is made of mahogany with the scale inscribed on an inset panel of boxwood. Courtesy: National Museum of History and Technology, Smithsonian Institution.

for his skills. The mathematical instruments commonly used by mapmakers and surveyors were the theodolite and the plain surveying compass, both of which were made of brass and suported in the field on wooden jacob staffs or tripods.

Brass as a material was as rare as the tropical woods in the colonies, or possibly more so, since all of the brass used in the New World until after the first quarter of the nineteenth century was imported from England in the form of ingots or sheets. The ingots were formed by being cast in sand, while sheets were made by pouring molten metal into forms made of slate shaped like large plates. The rough sheets produced were further reduced to specific thicknesses by beating with tilt hammers, usually water-powered. Some common utensils were formed directly from the brass plate by the same method.

These two forms of brass were shipped to the American colonies in the holds of ships, and the cost of transportation added to the original costs of production for the ingots or sheets made the metal excessively expensive. During the period between the beginning of the Revolution and the end of the War of 1812 importation of brass to America ceased almost completely, and the metal became all the more rare and costly. These conditions led colonial brassfounders and clockmakers to offer good prices for discarded brass and copper utensils and parts thereof, because they reused the metal by the process of "cementation," a technique first practiced in England in the sixteenth century. The broken-up pieces of discarded brass and copper were melted in crucibles with calamite or zinc carbonate, and the newly molten metal then poured into sand and slate molds in the forms desired. Zinc carbonate was a mineral mined in England in the form of lumps, which were ground into powder. It was, in fact, a form of the zinc metal. The English were most reluctant to share their monopoly or even to make available the raw brass they produced. The colonists had no American production of brass until zinc or tin was mined in adequate quantity in the New World, in the early decades of the nineteenth century.

It was this scarcity of the metal which led the early American

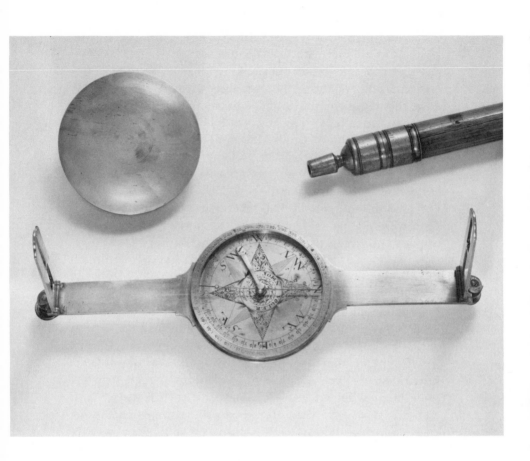

Brass surveying compass, shown with its cover and jacob
staff, made by John Vogler of Salem, North Carolina, late
eighteenth century. Courtesy: Old Salem, Inc.,
Winston-Salem, N. C.

instrument-maker to seek substitutes. Inasmuch as the basic element of all surveying instruments was the magnetic compass, hard metals other than brass could not be used. With characteristic ingenuity, the instrument-makers began to produce surveying compasses made of wood at considerably less cost than the same instruments made of brass. Frequently the same makers who made the instruments in metal produced their wooden counterparts as well.

The wooden surveying compass is one of the greatest curiosities in the history of the practical sciences in America as well as in the story of the skills that made America. Although it was produced and sold in quantity throughout the eighteenth century, historians of science as well as collectors and dealers were quite unaware of the existence of this type of instrument until approximately a decade ago. One example which had made its way into a major museum was considered at the time to be unique. Subsequent research brought to light occasional individual examples in other collections of historical societies, without acknowledgment or awareness of their purpose. When listed, if at all, they were generally identified as navigational instruments, purpose unknown. Not until an inventory was undertaken in recent years did an interest in these instruments develop; they were then identified as important tools of the early surveyors. This inventory made possible a comparative study to determine the variety in types, identity of makers, and other data.[7]

Wooden surveying compasses were produced by craftsmen who also made navigational instruments, as well as makers of brass surveying compasses, and some clockmakers. They were produced in wood for reasons of economy, the cost being but a fraction of what it would be in brass. Though used not only by the local surveyor engaged in laying out the property lines in his community, but occasionally by surveyors involved in more important endeavors, they were produced only in the New England colonies. For the most part they were used only in that region or regions where New England surveyors worked, such as the Ohio lands. Only an occasional example is the work

Wooden surveying compass apparently home-made and not
by a professional instrument-maker. The compass card,
hand-drawn in ink, with a colored North point, may be a
replacement for the original card. A pewter ring within the
circumference of the compass bowl is crudely stamped with
divisions for degrees, and every 10 degrees marked with
numbers. Courtesy: Mr. Preston R. Bassett, Ridgefield,
Connecticut.

of a Yankee whittler turned surveyor made for his own use; almost all of them are products of professional instrument-makers.

The wooden surveying compass was a very simple instrument. It consisted of a wooden body or plate formed with a round center, turned on the inner side to form a circular depression having a flat bottom and a ledge along its inner circumference. Two squared arms projected from the center with slots through the ends for the insertion of wooden sighting bars. Frequently a flat wooden block attached to the underside of the central body provided additional support. The woods used for these compasses were almost always native hardwoods, especially rock maple, apple, wild cherry, black walnut, birch, and hickory. Tropical woods were never employed except for the rare use of mahogany for a particularly fine example by a maker who specialized in navigational instruments. These were generally well finished and undoubtedly more costly.

An engraved paper compass card fitted snugly into the bottom of the circular portion, and a steel compass needle was seated upon a brass pivot at the center. A glass pane protected the card from the weather, and was fitted to the ledge provided for it and sealed with putty to make it dust-tight. The sighting bars were generally shaped from pear wood, apple or maple, perforated with slots having thread "hairs" held in place with tiny wooden plugs. The bars were readily removable for transportation. A flat cover made to protect the glass in the central portion in transit was invariably roughly shaped of pine and tied to the arms of the instrument by means of leather thongs.

A small number of the compasses presently known had other than engraved paper dials. The graduations were either painted along the circumference or stamped on an added pewter or brass ring. The majority of surviving examples utilized the engraved paper compass card made for the mariner's compass, which the same makers had engraved in quantity and used as needed. One characteristic that readily distinguished the original marine use of the card is that the East and West

Elaborate engraved compass card from a wooden surveying compass made of maple by Joseph Halsy (fl. 1697–1762) of Boston. The card is hand-colored in black, blue, red and gold with allegorical figures depicted within each of the cardinal points (Grammar, Logick, Geometry, Arithmetick, Astronomy, Rhetorick and Musick). A sailing vessel under a crescent moon is featured in the central medallion.
Courtesy: New Hampshire Historical Society.

points remain as they are found in the standard compass rose, and were not reversed in accordance with common surveying practice.

Rare examples exist in which the compass rose was inked by hand, usually crudely, on paper or a painted surface. These were probably replacements for a lost or damaged original card, although one or two may have been the original works of a whittler or home workshop.

Generally the wooden surveying compass was simply and sturdily constructed, without any of the decorative touches that rendered artistic satisfaction to the artisan. A seasoned block of wood was selected, planed flat, and then the form required was scribed with a carpenter's compass, first for the circular body, and then a center line was drawn through the circle and along both arms, followed by lines for the width dimension of the arms. The finished body was smoothed throughout, although the center lines generally remained visible. The only decorative element was the compass card. The putty into which the glass was set was generally tinted with red pigment, to provide a finished appearance to the completed instrument.

The decorative elements of the compass cards featured in both the marine compass and surveying compass deserve some comment. A dominant large central boss was illustrated with an appropriate figure, scene, or motif which distinguished the maker's interests. In examples produced before the Revolution these ranged from the English tudor rose, the figure of Britannia, to the three royal feathers, and an English crown. A favorite subject was a shipmaster on shore using a backstaff.

After the middle of the eighteenth century, the motifs associated with the mother country were discarded and more innocuous subjects were featured, such as the figure of Neptune, a lighthouse, a ship at sea, or a foliated design. The American eagle, which in the earlier designs was a particularly ugly bird, came more and more into use as a decorative motif, not only for compass cards but on trade cards as well. Other makers used the central boss to inscribe their own name and business address.

Not all of the instruments used by the practitioners were made by the professional instrument-makers, however. Occasionally, a locally appointed surveyor in a small New England inland community did not have the resource of an instrument-maker in the area, and had to provide for his own needs. Based on his self-taught rudimentary knowledge of the subject, he would while away the winter hours in creating an instrument of his own design. Generally these were not copied from existing instruments but conceived directly from the purpose that the instrument was required to fulfill; the surveyor utilized his own skills and materials to fashion what he required. A few of these home-made instruments which have survived are worthy of comment.

One example, resembling a brass theodolite, was found in a barn in Vermont. The maker is not known, but the instrument remains a monument to his ingenuity. It features a hollowed-out telescopic tube without lenses for sighting, makeshift leveling devices, and a compass dial stamped in pewter and having a steel compass needle. The instrument is extremely adaptable and reflects not only considerable calculation but experience as well.

Another example is a vertical level made of hickory with a vertical pewter scale, and a plummet level suspended from the top center. An interesting feature is that the pewter scale is chamfered on both edges so that it fits firmly in place. The instrument had the customary simple wooden sighting bars, now missing, that slipped into place at each end, and was equipped with an unusual leveling device. A bubble level was installed along the top surface of the instrument and brass-set-screws were installed in such a manner that the instrument could be fixed and maintained level by manipulating the screws with the fingers. An opening for a large wooden screw at the center presumably attached a plain wooden cover over the scale to protect it in travel.

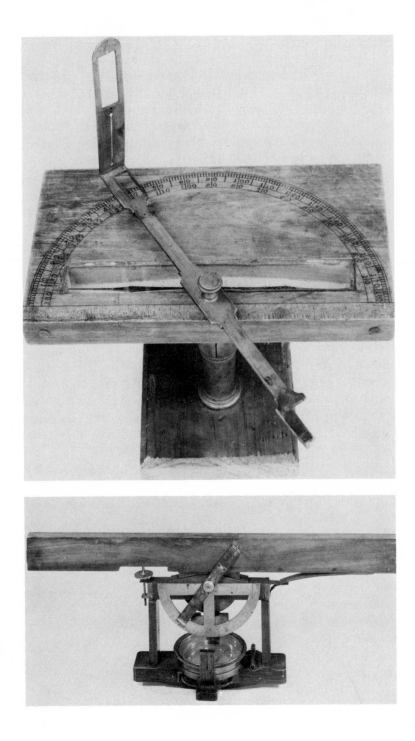

Wooden semi-circumferentor (left top) made in New England, late eighteenth century, by an unknown maker. One sighting bar is broken. Courtesy: Maine Historical Society, Portland, Maine.

Wooden surveying compendium, (left bottom) late eighteenth or early nineteenth century, maker not known. The telescopic tube of hollowed wood can be adjusted for elevation by means of a spring and set-screw and the lower component is a surveying compass with wooden sighting bars and a pewter compass dial and bubbel level. The instrument was readily dismantled for transporting. Courtesy: Mr. Robert Elea, Boston, Mass.

Wooden surveying instrument made of hickory (above), late eighteenth century, maker not known. Sighting bars, now missing, were inserted at terminals of upper bar and fixed at desired inclination by means of set screws. A pewter strip is engraved with a scale inscribed to 90° in both directions from the center; a bubble level is provided on the upper surface, and a lead plummet is used against the scale on the face of the instrument. Private collection.

A significant aspect of the wooden surveying instruments is that they were produced only in New England, presumably from the early eighteenth century through the first quarter of the nineteenth century. Although makers of the wooden instruments of navigation were prevalent in New York City, Philadelphia, and Baltimore, as well as other major ports of the Middle Colonies during the same period, and despite the fact that there was considerable need for surveying instruments in these regions as well, there is no evidence that any of them produced wooden instruments for surveying.

The possible relationship between the makers of wooden scientific instruments and New England confirms the particular affinity for wood and its applications in that region. Curiously, no substantial link has been found between the makers of wooden instruments and the makers of wooden clocks, however, although some of the clockmakers also produced brass surveying instruments. There are fewer of these than might be expected, and they generally made surveying instruments in brass, not wood.[8]

Wood as the material for scientific instruments was not limited only to the needs of navigation and surveying, but was also used for some of the instruments for teaching science in academies and colleges. Notable among these were globes and orreries used in teaching geography and astronomy. The first maker of globes in America was James Wilson, a Vermont farmer who saw his first globe during a visit to a friend at Dartmouth College in 1795.[9] Back on the farm he determined to duplicate the instrument, and was able eventually to purchase a copy of the *Encyclopedia Britannica* on the installment plan by selling several cows. After studying terrestrial and celestial maps in this source, he walked to Boston to visit Jedediah Morse, author of the first American geography texts, in the hope that the latter would instruct him in geography. Failing to enlist Morse's interest, he then made his way on foot to New Haven to learn the art of engraving with Amos Doolittle.

Wilson's first globes were solid spheres turned in wood,

Terrestrial globe made by James Wilson in 1831.
Courtesy: Explorers Hall, the National Geographic Society,
Washington, D. C.

which he then covered with layers of paper glued one on top of the other. The surface was made smooth and then the gores were applied. These he had drawn and engraved himself. Wilson subsequently made his globes of hollow paper shells he learned to produce over a turned wooden core. He also turned the pedestals and frames in wood on a turning lathe in his barn. From this small beginning he developed a market which enabled him to establish a successful factory in Albany, later conducted by his sons and then by his son-in-law. It continued in business until about 1855. The Wilson globes became popular throughout America and sold rapidly, because they were accurate, up-to-date, and less expensive than those imported from England and France.

Globes were occasionally produced in America as unique examples for limited use, such as one turned in a solid wooden sphere and mounted on a bench by Samuel Lane. The local cobbler and surveyor of Stratham, New Hampshire, he used the globe in connection with his surveys. It was not until after the first quarter of the nineteenth century that other American makers began to produce globes, chiefly for use in schools.

Other science-teaching instruments constructed of wood were rules and gauging rods, electrostatic machines having a wooden framework, and gunnery gauges. Teaching devices for astronomy, such as orreries, were generally produced in metal and imported from England, except for rare examples. An astronomical apparatus constructed entirely in wood which may be unique recently came to light in New England. On the basis of present study, this instrument was probably produced in Massachusetts between 1780 and 1812. Designed to be used probably by a traveling lecturer, it could readily be dismantled for transporting and was easily reassembled. It consists of two major components, the first of which is a hand-driven mechanism demonstrating the motion of the moon around the earth, and of the earth and other planets around the sun. This was inserted into a socket in the table by means of a peg pinned into place. The table legs, which are later replacements, slid into slots and could be easily removed so that the

Portable table orrery made entirely of wood with brass and pewter components, late eighteenth or early nineteenth century, maker unknown. The orrery is operated by hand motion moving the wheelwork along the table surface. The upper plate of the wheelwork is decorated with painted representations of the sun, moon and a comet. Courtesy: National Museum of History and Technology, Smithsonian Institution.

hinged tabletop could be folded. The tabletop was decorated with the figures of the zodiac, and the upper surface of the geared assembly was decorated with representations of the sun, the moon, and a comet. A gilt metallic paint was used and the delineations appear to be copies of the crude representations from the almanacs of the period.

The apparatus differs from other orreries presently known in that it is neither crank-driven nor clock-driven, as in all other examples. Instead, it is hand-operated, accomplished by moving the geared assembly along the circumference of the table, so that it was truly a demonstrational device. The orreries produced in America prior to the end of the first quarter of the nineteenth century were few in number, the work of David Rittenhouse, Joseph Pope, Aaron Willard, Jr., or James Wilson, the globe maker. Wilson produced several orreries in his later years for Vermont academies, none of which is presently known.[10] This apparatus may be one of them, but it is most likely that it was made by or for Bartholomew Burges of Boston (ca. 1740–1807). In 1789 Burges published a small treatise on "The Solar System Displayed," illustrated with an engraved chart, a work which not only presented an account of the solar system but was concerned as well with Halley's Comet, expected to appear again in the spring of that year.[11] Early in 1789 Burges advertised in the Boston press a lecture and demonstration of "An Astronomical Apparatus," and the possibility exists that it may in fact have been this one.[12] Not only is this apparatus an ingenious science-teaching device, but it is a superlative example of the replacement of metal by wood for the construction of scientific instruments by the colonial American craftsman.

The instrument-maker had a substantial role in his community and the nature of his work ensured his position as a member of the middle class. As one of the skilled artisans, he was on the same social level as the silversmith, the clockmaker, and other skilled craftsmen as distinct from the merchant or members of the trades. They were generally men of substance, owning properties other than their own homes and shops. They were important members of their church councils, and were often appointed to positions of responsibility in their communities. Many of them were members of colonial families with distinguished descendants in later generations.

A characteristic which they shared with other members of the skilled crafts was their pride in their specialty, and they proudly announced themselves on their shop signs, trade cards, and newspaper advertisement as "makers of mathematical instruments." Although modern historians have suggested that this form of nomenclature was developed in modern times, such was indeed not the case.[13]

A characteristic of the colonial American instrument-maker that distinguished him from his English counterpart was that in America he generally worked as an individual, without membership in a trade organization or association with others engaged in the same craft. The colonists found it impossible to adopt the philosophy and organization implicit in the guild system, for the American way of life was predicated on freedom of thought and action, and the craftsman was rarely bound by the rigid requirements that restrained his counterparts in the Old World. Furthermore, in the colonies there was a great scarcity of skilled labor, and a considerable potential for work was available even to those without craft credentials.

In England quite the opposite condition prevailed. The numbers of young men seeking work of all types, and particularly desiring respectable careers in the crafts, made it possible to impose many restrictions upon the crafts in the form of regulations directed through the agency of the guilds. Guilds had the responsibility for overseeing the quality of training of the apprentices as well as for providing standards of workmanship. They were furthermore required to police their operation and oversee the quality of products. Under this system each artisan was limited to work only within his selected and announced specialty regardless of the condition of the market for it, and whether he was particularly qualified for his craft. If in time the apprentice discovered another type of work to which he was better suited, or that he preferred, he was restrained within the regulations of his guild.

In the New World attempts to establish a guild system succeeded in some trades and crafts, at least for periods of time. In other skilled employment, however, they did not succeed at all. The primary reason for failure of the system was the limited amount of labor available to the considerable demand for men in many skills. With the urgent market for the products of all the trades and crafts, there was not sufficient time to wait for formalized training of apprentices. Even if and when it was possible to do so, the nature of the colonial American was such that he was not content to wait, and would not tolerate regulations that forced him to do so. Frequently when a novice learning the craft of the instrument-maker or clockmaker had mastered the basic rudiments of the art, gained a working knowledge of the use of the tools, and achieved sufficient familiarity with the work to the degree that he could undertake repairs or do the most important part of the work, he became impatient to launch out for himself independently, and would not await the completion of the term of apprenticeship. The need was greater than the supply throughout this period, and there was no lack of work for even semi-skilled hands.

In the colonies the shortage of labor was so critical that the master craftsman often was willing to take on an apprentice without a cash endowment, with the agreement to feed, house, and train him, and provide a nominal education by enrolling him in evening schools. As an added inducement, the apprenticeship term was frequently shortened from seven years to not more than four or five years. Even so, it was difficult to entice enough young boys to the trades and crafts of their own volition.

When the guild system or the practice of apprenticeship succeeded, as it did occasionally, it was primarily because it was the most important of the existing local educational institutions, and was subsidized by the community on that basis. Two types of apprenticeship were common in New England in the colonial period. The first was the traditional "voluntary" form, by means of which a candidate for apprenticeship bound himself to a master craftsman of his own will for the prescribed period because he was eager to learn and practice a trade. Parents generally paid a specified amount of money for the privilege of having a son trained, and in return the master would provide board, lodging, training and minimum schooling.

The other source for apprentices was "compulsory." Illegitimate or orphaned children without family support, or other town charges, were bound out by community officials to live with master craftsmen, who agreed not only to provide room, board, and clothing, but also to train them in their own trade in addition to providing them with an elementary education, either in their home or outside. Reading and writing were basic requirements, for example, and when the craftsman was unable to furnish such schooling because of his own illiteracy, he was obliged to send the apprentice at his own expense to the local schoolmaster or to someone who could teach him.

Another small source of apprentices was derived from the requirement under the colonial law that everyone must be engaged in some form of useful occupation if he did not have an estate sufficient for his maintenance.[14] The community played an important role in this system, for the selectmen, churchwardens and other town officials were obliged to serve as overseers to ensure not only that the master was fulfilling his obligations, but that the youth was at the same time performing in accordance to his contract.

When an apprentice had completed his period of training and fulfilled his obligations, he received two sets of apparel from the master, his indenture was duly recorded as having been completed, and he was then free to ply his trade as a journeyman wherever he wished. If he were particularly competent, the master might offer him the opportunity to work in his shop at an established rate of pay. More frequently the newly graduated craftsman was anxious to break away and seek his fortune in other communities. If, as was often the case, he had been engaged and was anxious for marriage, he might marry and remain with his former master until he had put aside a modest sum needed to establish his own shop in the same community or in another town. Just as frequently, a particularly capable young artisan might be enticed into the shop of his former master's competitor, because of the ever-increasing need for skilled hands.

The apprenticeship system worked relatively well in some of the trades and crafts but less so in the more skilled occupations such as the clockmakers and makers of mathematical instruments. In these, it was customary to employ shop assistants or clerks and errand boys, and apprentices were infrequently trained. In those instances of which a record has survived, the apprentice was generally a son, nephew, or other relative. The reason for the lack of a training program in the more skilled crafts is not known, but a possible reason may be the fact that these crafts were often part-time, and a future in their pursuit was not as assured as careers in other fields. Another factor may have been the necessity for the additional skill of engraving, which might have required further training with another master. Such training would be costly and time-consuming without the assurance of an adequate trade. It was difficult for the instrument-maker to compete for promising young assistants against the many opportunities that were being offered in other crafts that promised more income and less drudgery.

A sufficient number of professionally trained instrument-makers who served apprenticeship are known to allow the assumption that the practice was followed in the colonies, but only as and when it was practical to do so, and generally with members of the craftsman's family.

The shop of the instrument-maker was a focus for the shipping world in maritime communities. The shop sign, usually "At The Sign of the Quadrant," served as a beacon for shipmasters coming into port, for local seafarers about to undertake a voyage, and for merchants, shipowners and others of the community who shared maritime concerns. The instrument-

The "Little Navigator" shop figure made of polychromed wood American, eighteenth century. The figure was used in front of the shop of James A. Fales in Providence, Rhode Island and later in New Bedford, Massachusetts. Courtesy: Old Dartmouth Historical Society and Whaling Museum, New Bedford, Mass.

maker's shop in that period was more than merely a working place. In it the instrument-maker also stocked and sold charts, almanacs, and nautical texts. In addition to the shop facilities, it also incorporated a storeroom or warehouse, or even a ship's chandlery where ship's supplies could be purchased in quantity sufficient for a voyage. In a period when banks, labor exchanges, and insurance companies were not as prevalent as they became during the later nineteenth century, the instrument-maker's shop often included some of these services as well.

The New England instrument-maker's affinity for wood was represented even in his advertising. Prior to the advent of newspapers, the only means of advertising the skills and products of the trades and crafts were shop signs. The flat sign bearing the owner's name, craft, and products was traditionally displayed over the shop entrance or sometimes suspended from a projecting arm over the street from the corner of the building. The signs reflected the tradition and pride of the craftsman much more than representing an effort to purvey a skill or a product. The signs of the instrument-maker frequently incorporated a symbolic device representing the most common product.

Gradually craftsmen on both sides of the Atlantic added another dimension to their advertising, in the form of a shop figure. These were three-dimensional representations of a human figure holding a product or other object associated with the business being conducted in the shop. The most frequent examples, and readily identifiable, were the ship's figurehead which stood at the door of the ship's carver, and later the so-called cigar-store Indian holding tobacco leaves or cigars advertising the tobacconist, which were common even into our own time. The symbol most frequently used by makers of mathematical instruments was the figure of a shipmaster or mariner holding a quadrant. Such figures were commonly used equally by makers and dealers in mathematical instruments in England as well as in the major New England port cities in the eighteenth and early nineteenth centuries.

Probably the earliest surviving American example of the instrument-maker's shop figures is the one known as "The Little Admiral," which was a favorite landmark on Boston's Long Wharf for more than a century and a half. It is believed to have first identified Admiral Vernon's Tavern, and from about 1750 it marked the shop of the instrument-maker, William Williams, and then of his successor, Samuel Thaxter. It is claimed that the figure was carved by Simeon Skillin, a carver who achieved considerable fame with his figureheads and shop figures. The date 1770 which the figure bears coincides with the date when Williams opened his shop on King Street. The figure continued to designate the instrument-maker's shop, then known as Thaxter and Son, until it went out of business in 1916. A second figure used by Samuel Thaxter to identify his shop was Father Time, a figure carved for him by John Skillin late in the eighteenth century and used at first as a decoration inside Thaxter's shop.[15]

Similar carved figures were used by other instrument-makers, including Samuel King of Newport. King's figure of a little mariner may have been the same which was later acquired and used by James Fales, Jr., of the same city. Fales subsequently moved to New Bedford, Massachusetts, and when his shop was abandoned in 1888, the figure was acquired for and preserved at the Whaling Museum.[16]

Simeon Skillin was probably the carver also of the "Winged Mercury" that was featured outside the Boston Post Office on State Street early in the nineteenth century. It was acquired by Frederick W. Lincoln after 1850 and installed at his shop, identified as "At the Sign of the Mercury and Quadrant."

Nautical shop figures of the instrument-makers were prevalent first in New England shipping communities, and were to be found in other shipping centers such as New York or Philadelphia after the beginning of the nineteenth century. They had all disappeared from the scene by the turn of the present century, except for one notable example, which identified the shop of Riggs & Bros. in Philadelphia, makers of mathematical instruments and repairers of chronometers. The

"Father Time," late eighteenth century shop figure carved by John Skillin of Boston for Samuel Thaxter for use in his shop on State Street. The scythe is broken. Courtesy: Bostonian Society.

firm was established in Philadelphia in 1818, and continued in business until 1973.

The application of wood to the needs of the practical sciences spanned the existence of the mathematical practitioner movement in America, from the seventeenth century to the end of the first quarter of the nineteenth century, and having achieved its purpose, came to an end with the movement's demise.

The wooden instruments of science fulfilled the immediate needs of the mathematical practitioners, but they accomplished even more. Their production contributed in at least a small degree to the evolution of a new art form that was totally American and distinguished by its severe simplicity of form and decoration. Finally, they contributed to familiarization by the public with things scientific in a period when science was new.[17]

Colonial Watermills In the Wooden Age

Charles Howell

To THE FIRST European settlers in North America, and in particular to the more mechanically minded, the sight of the numerous rushing rivers and tumbling creeks must have instantly brought thoughts of the abundant waterpower which was available for harnessing. Readily available power would ease the laborious tasks of providing food, shelter, and clothing that had to be performed by hand to sustain life in the untamed lands of the New World.

Millions of acres of North America were covered with virgin forests; before any quantity of food crops could be grown, much of these forests had to be cleared. Besides clearing the land for agriculture, the felled lumber produced an abundant source of raw material for building homes, barns, and mills. For the important task of harnessing the waterpower, timber was available for constructing dams, waterwheels, gearing, and power-transmission shafts.

From somewhat sketchy records it appears that the first waterwheels provided the power for sawmills. There were abundant supplies of lumber long before there was any quantity of grain available for the use of cereal-grinding mills, or gristmills as they were usually termed. Apart from the plentiful supply of timber for sawing, the beams, planks, and boards produced by the sawmills were of immense value to the colonists for trade.

Another important commodity to the colonists was iron—to manufacture implements, tools, nuts and bolts, and for certain working parts of mills, such as waterwheel gudgeons, shaft collars, and other small fittings. Since in the beginning all this essential iron had to be imported from Europe, it became important to establish ironworks in America. From quite early colonial days, water was used extensively to power ironworks. The best-known example is the Saugus Iron Works in Massachusetts, which became operational about 1646 and has now been completely restored. In addition to sawmills, gristmills, and ironworks, waterpower was used to prepare wool and plant fibers for the making of cloth. However, we are here primarily concerned with waterpowered colonial gristmills.

Probably the first grinding of grain by waterpower in the North American colonies utilized very primitive methods, largely influenced by the type of mills used in the countries of origin of the settlers. Many of these mills were so small and simple that their existence went unrecorded. In the South it is known that "plumping mills" were utilized. A mill of this kind was simply a long tree sweep, centrally pivoted on forked branches. At one end of the sweep was fastened a wooden box which was filled by a small stream of water from a wooden trough. When the box was full, the weight forced the sweep downwards; the box emptied on descent, thereby releasing the weight. The box end of the sweep then swung back again to the filling position due to a counterweight at the opposite end of the sweep. The counterweight was a piece of hardwood shaped like a pestle. When dropped suddenly because of the release of the water in the box, it would fall into a hardwood mortar in which the grain was placed. The constant rise and fall of the hardwood pestle, caused by the water filling and emptying the box, pounded the grain into meal. This method of grinding can still be seen in presentday Brazil.

Although we have little documentary evidence, the first rotary type of watermill in North America was probably of the "Greek" or "Norse" types. The first historical reference to such mills, the first rotary mills to be powered by water, dates from about 85 B.C. in Greece, although they may have originated in Asia minor. These were simple horizontal mills, easily adapted to drive the small hand-operated millstones or querns of the first settlers.

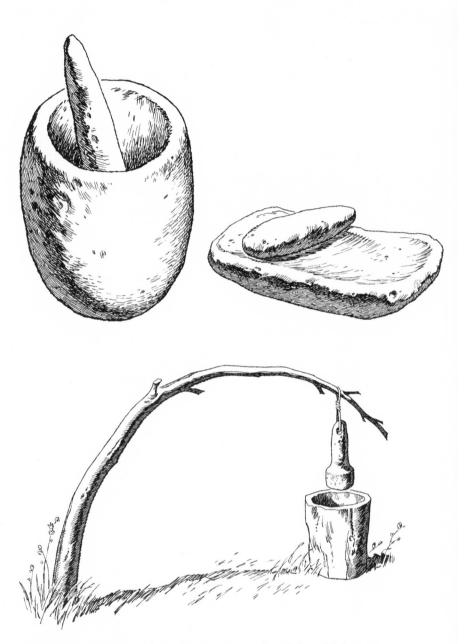

Primitive methods of grinding grain utilized hand labor. At the top left is a mortar and pestle; at the right is a saddle stone and metate, in which a roller stone is used to crush the grain. Below is an early plumping mill, which utilized a long tree sweep.

This horizontal wheel, shown at rest, is located in Lemiro Carvide, Portugal. Photo: Rex Wailes.

A horizontal mill wheel from Alcobaca, Portugal, about 46 cm. in diameter, bonded with iron. The wheel, of the "Greek" type found in warmer climates, has spoon-shaped blades. The blades of the "Norse" wheel were flatter in shape so that ice would not form. Photo: Rex Wailes.

Because this primitive horizontal mill was reasonably cheap and simple to construct and had no gearing, it was well suited to be built by small pioneering communities and would easily grind enough meal to supply their immediate needs. This simple horizontal mill was made almost entirely of wood, and consisted of a hub or "boss" into which were morticed a number of blades or vanes varying in shape according to the individual ideas of the builders.

The shaft, which could be of wood or iron, passed vertically upward through a wooden bearing in the center of the lower millstone and was fixed to the upper millstone, which revolved with the waterwheel. The millstream was channeled into an inclined wood or stone trough arranged so as to discharge a jet of water against the blades and so turn the wheel and the upper stone. Below the wheel, there was a simple thrust bearing, into which ran the end of the shaft. This bearing thus carried the weight of the shaft, the wheel, and the upper millstone. The bearing was usually mounted on a beam or bridgetree, which could be raised or lowered to adjust the clearance between the stones and produce finer or coarser meal as required. A square wooden hopper shaped like an inverted pyramid was positioned above the upper stone, the grain fed from the base of the hopper into a tapering wooden trough called a "shoe." The shoe was continuously vibrated by various types of eccentric devices that were turned or agitated by the upper stone, causing the grain to trickle into the center hole or "eye" of the revolving stone. The grain passed between the stones and was ground into meal, which emerged all around the periphery of the stones and was trapped in the wooden case or "tun." The revolving upper stone carried the meal around to the spout hole, where it was discharged.

The Swedish settlers in the Brandywine Valley, Delaware, used the Norse type of mill on tributary streams. An example of a horizontal mill can be seen in the Doylestown Museum, Bucks County, Pennsylvania. The restored San José Mission, San Antonio, Texas, also has an example of a horizontal-type mill, undoubtedly reflecting the Spanish influence. Even today, in several parts of the Iberian Peninsula horizontal mills are still at work, and there are hundreds more still in active operation in some of the mountainous areas of Latin America. The buildings that house these mills are little more than tiny log cabins; and it can be assumed that the first waterpowered mills used by the North American colonists were in similar primitive structures.

The primitive horizontal mills led to development of the tub wheel, basically the same as the horizontal wheel, except that it ran in a circular wood enclosure, like a tub without a bottom. From a flume or sluiceway, a downwardly inclined, enclosed wooden trough or penstock was tapered inwardly toward the delivery point and directed the water in a jet against the blades of the wheel. The protruding sides of the tub formed a continuous apron to prevent the water from escaping sideways, which improved the efficiency of the wheel. In some applications the "tub" was of masonry, with the wheel revolving within a cylindrical well of stone blocks. In somewhat improved later designs the blades were often set at an angle so as to be more nearly perpendicular to the column of water flowing against them. Some of the wheels were fitted with a shrouded broad rim that became the tub or apron and revolved as an integral part of the wheel. The early tub wheels drove millstones on exactly the same principle as the horizontal mill, the upper millstone being directly attached to the shaft of the wheel.

In later versions of the tub wheel, some were fitted with spur wheels attached to the shaft so that more than one pair of millstones could be driven, and at an increased speed to the waterwheel. Although tub wheels were highly inefficient, they were extensively used and in isolated cases their use has continued until modern times. A good example of an original gristmill driven by tub wheels with gearing can be seen at Oakdale, Long Island, New York. There are scant remains of three wooden tub wheels, but the sturdy oak wheelshafts are still complete. Two of the wheels each drove a single pair of stones by spur gears, which have been modernized by the use of cast iron. The third wheel drove all the ancillary machinery,

The shaft of an early American tub wheel at the Southside Sportsmen's Club, Connetquot River State Park, Oakdale, Long Island. The photo was taken prior to restoration.

A reconstructed tub wheel at Old Sturbridge Village, Sturbridge, Mass. Photo: Donald F. Eaton.

which comprised the grain cleaners, the flour-dressing reels, and a sack hoist.

Although the Norse mills and tub wheels were used in many colonial settlements because of their simplicity and relatively low cost, the more efficient vertical waterwheels with horizontal driveshafts were much more widely used. These waterwheels were of four main types—(1) overshot; (2) pitchback; (3) breastshot (low, middle, or high); and (4) undershot—the names indicating the point on the wheel at which the water was fed to it. If the wheel is regarded as a clock face, with the water coming to it from the left, then the overshot wheel is fed at about 12:30 or 1 o'clock, the pitchback at about 11 or 11:30, the breastshot at between 8 and 10:30, and the undershot at about 7 o'clock. In these examples, with the water coming in from the left, the overshot would revolve clockwise, and the three other types counterclockwise.

Throughout the colonial period these vertical waterwheels were almost completely built of wood and had five main parts: (1) the shaft, (2) arms, (3) shrouding or rims, (4) the sole or drum boards, and (5) the partitions which formed the buckets or floats. The shafts were almost universally of oak, those used in gristmills usually being from 18 to 24 inches in diameter, dressed in a circular, polygonal, or square form, and fitted with iron bands around them. In the ends of the shafts iron gudgeons were inserted, so that the protruding ends of the gudgeons ran on the bearings. Bearings were often of stone, but wood and brass were also used. In some cases water was used to lubricate the stone bearing, particularly on the outside waterwheel bearing. A small wooden spout conducted a trickle of water on to the revolving gudgeon to give constant lubrication; rendered animal fats were also used as lubrication on all these types of early bearings. The type of wheel used depended on the head or fall of water available and on the mill site in general. Most of the wheels were designed by the skilled millwrights who built them. The majority of early colonial waterwheels were comparatively small in diameter, often between 10 and

15 feet. Later colonial wheels were much larger and more powerful.

Overshot wheels were employed at most heads of water over 10 feet. The water was conveyed to the top of the wheel by a wooden trough or flume and fed into the buckets. These buckets were formed by boards set at an angle toward the stream, and the ends of the boards were set into slots in the shrouds or rims of the wheel. The depth of the shrouds varied, but was usually 9 to 15 inches. The bottom edges of the buckets were fastened to the sole or drum formed by planks secured to the inside edge of the shrouds. Wheels of this type of construction were often referred to as "bucket wheels." Power generated by overshot wheels depends almost entirely on the weight of water in the buckets, but the forward momentum of the water as it enters the buckets adds a slight increment to their power.

A variation to the overshot waterwheel was the pitchback wheel, in which the water was conveyed to the top, or almost to the top, of the wheel by a flume. The buckets in the pitchback were set at an angle opposite to those in an overshot. The end of the flume and the control gate or shut were adapted so that the water fed downward into the buckets at the reverse direction to the flow of the stream, causing the pitchback wheel to revolve in the opposite direction. There was an arc of stone or wood, known as an apron, usually of the same radius as the wheel. The edge of the buckets ran close to this apron, to confine the water and prevent it from spilling from the buckets before arriving at the lowest point of the fall. An efficient type of apron would terminate with a step downward of about 6 inches, usually about a foot before the lowest point of the run. This enabled the water to be discharged rapidly from the buckets, so as not to impede the upward motion of the wheel. Like overshot wheels, pitchbacks derived most of their power from the weight of the water in the buckets, but received a certain amount of additional impulse from the water as it fed in from the flume.

Breast waterwheels, most commonly used at falls of between 6 and 10 feet, were of construction similar to overshot and

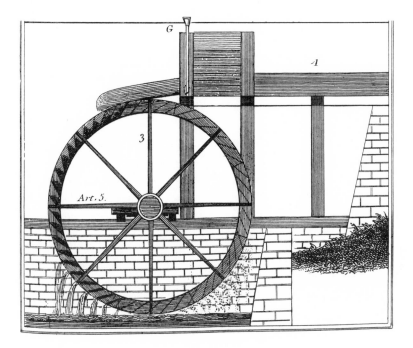

Oliver Evans illustrated his book *The Young Mill-Wright and Miller's Guide* (Philadelphia, 1795) with 28 descriptive plates. This drawing portrays an overshot wheel, in which the "water is laid on at the top."

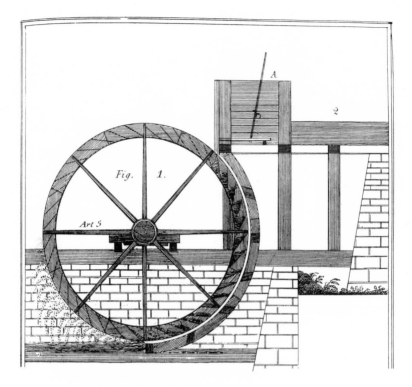

"Pitch-back wheels are constructed exactly similar to breast wheels, only the water is struck on them at a greater height," advised Oliver Evans. This drawing shows a pitchback wheel 18 ft. in diameter.

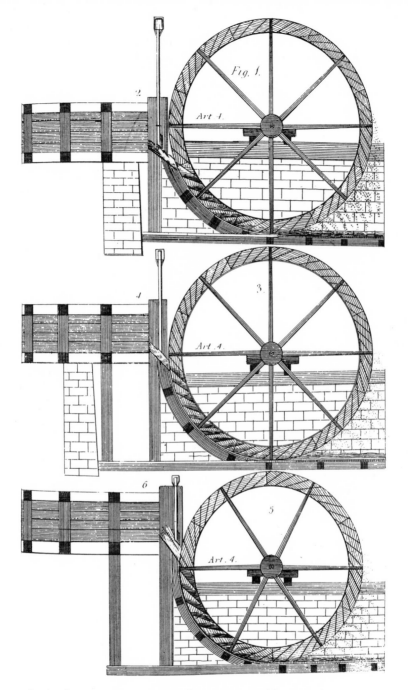

These drawings represent three types of breast wheels—from top to bottom, a low, middle, and high wheel. Evans said, "Breast wheels differ but little in their structure or material from overshot, excepting only that the water passes under instead of over them and they must be wider in proportion as their fall is less."

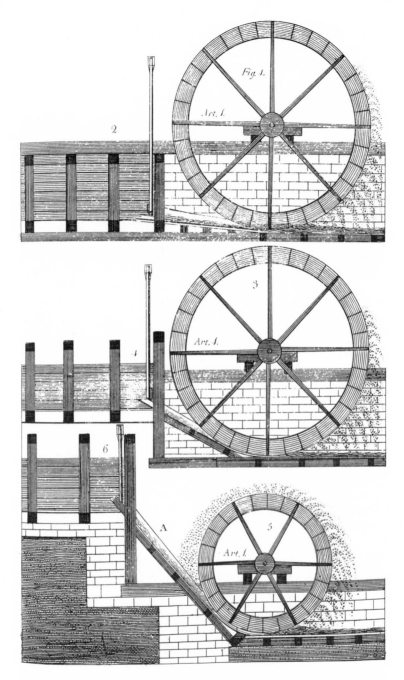

Three types of undershot wheels are shown here in drawings from Evans' guidebook. In each the water strikes the wheel at a different point. Evans warned, "This wheel requires more water than a breast-mill, with the same fall."

pitchback wheels. Aprons were usually fitted to retain the water in the same type of enclosed buckets as in the case of the pitchback wheels. In middle and low breast wheels, the buckets were deeper, to deal with the increased volume of water required for the low head of water to develop power equivalent to that obtained by a high breast wheel. Breast wheels combined both the weight and impluse of the water for their operation, and well-designed wheels of this type were very popular.

For low falls of water undershot wheels were employed. These wheels were moved entirely by the impulse of the water and consequently required much greater quantities of water to produce the same power as developed by the overshot, pitchback, or breast wheels. In construction the undershot wheels differed little from the bucket-type wheels, except that the buckets were replaced by radial floats. The early undershot wheels usually had floats constructed of flat boards with no right-angle back or sole boards on the inside rim of the wheel, but some later wheels increased efficiency by having these backs fitted to prevent the water from shooting over the floats. In some undershot wheels the floats were fitted into slots in deep shrouds or rims. In other wheels the rims were not so deep but were of thicker timber, which was morticed and had short protruding arms, or "starts," driven into them to which the floats were fastened. Water was admitted to undershot wheels by a sluice gate, called a "shut." At its base this would be set as close as possible to the wheel, on such an angle that its top moved away from the wheel; in this way the shut acted as a conductor, guiding the water in a downward path to strike the floats in the operative direction of the wheel. Undershot wheels ran in an enclosed channel, which in early colonial mills was built of either wood or stone. The base of the channel formed a close-fitting apron as in the case of the pitchback and breast wheels. Ordinarily undershot wheels were built from about 10 to 25 feet in diameter. The floats were from 14 to 16 inches apart at the circumference, and about 12 to 28 inches in depth.

The relative efficiency of the various types of waterwheels was long a matter of speculation and controversy; but, of course, the efficiency of all the wheels depended on the head of water available, that is, the difference in level between the water feeding the wheel (the "head" water) and that leaving it (the "tail" water). The greater the head of water, the larger the wheel could be and the more numerous the buckets. The overshot and pitchback wheels needed the greatest head of water and were the most efficient, for a larger number of buckets were filled at one time. For the same reasons a high breast wheel was more efficient than a middle or low breast wheel. In turn, the middle and low breast wheels were more efficient than the undershot wheels.

For maximum efficiency it was essential in all waterwheel installations that the tail water leave the wheel quickly. The construction of good free-flowing tailraces was very important. In early colonial mills the tailrace was often built up of planks laid in the direction of the stream and supported by sills; these planked tailraces also protected the bed of the stream from being washed away. Stone was also used to construct tailraces, usually depending upon which construction material was most available.

Various kinds of timber were used for the waterwheels. Some were made completely of oak, others had an oak shaft, but had arms, soling, and buckets made from other kinds of timber. Pine of certain types was found to be fairly long-lasting in waterwheels, but cypress was perhaps the best rot-resisting wood discovered for waterwheel construction. Although wooden waterwheels were always strongly made, exposure to water, ice, snow, and sun shortened the active life of the wood, and repairs were frequently necessary. In a period of five to ten years, almost every part of a wooden wheel, except the main shaft, would have to be repaired or replaced.

Some of the early mills were erected on natural waterfalls; but at most mill sites it was essential to build a dam to obtain the necessary head of water. To withstand the considerable pressure of the water, the dams and weirs had to be solidly constructed. Some consisted of continuous stone-filled cribbing of rough-hewn oak, pine, or locust logs, which were usually more than 9 inches square with each piece notched into those above and below. This cribbing supported a series of strongbacks, spaced about 4 feet, 6 inches apart, of both rough and hewn logs which were mostly around 10 inches in diameter. These strongbacks were laid parallel to the axis of the stream and at about a 45 degree angle, with the apex upstream and a double thickness of 1-inch planking nailed to them. There were, of course, many different ways of constructing timber dams, and many were constructed of logs and stone combined. Other dams were built completely of rocks or stone, which might be "laid dry" or with mortar, or perhaps bolted with iron bars.

From the dam to the mill, the water flowed through a headrace, which was sometimes of considerable length. The final channel through which the water flowed before reaching the wheel, the flume or sluiceway, was often of timber construction. Wooden flumes were usually a box section with plank sides and bottom supported on masonry piers, wood cribbing, or piles. The longitudinal members, or "rangers," were notched into the flume sills and the bearers above the piers of piles; all were spiked solidly together.

The rise and fall of the tide was used to power many mills. These were usually built on the estuaries of shallow creeks, with the dams constructed to form a millpond by holding the water back at high tide. In most cases a hinged sluice gate in the dam would be forced open by the incoming tide and would thus fill the pond. As the tide began to flow out, it would close the sluice gate, thereby trapping the water at high level in the pond. When the tide had gone out sufficiently, a head of water was available to power a waterwheel. The operation of these mills was confined to two periods in 24 hours, each about 5½ hours; and, of course, these periods came at various times in a 24-hour period. The thrifty Dutch settlers soon recognized the potential of the powerful tides running into the creeks of New Amsterdam; and by 1636 a miller named Gerritson was operat-

The wooden raceway and wheel at the reconstructed
Philipsburg Manor, Upper Mills, North Tarrytown,
New York.

ing a tidal mill in Midwout, now Flatbush. This mill survived until modern times.

In order for vertical waterwheels mounted on horizontal shafts to drive millstones, it was necessary to change the direction of the drive through 90 degrees. Gearing was introduced for this purpose. It was first developed by the Romans in the type of watermill described by Vitruvius between 20 and 11 B.C.

In the early colonial gristmills each waterwheel was geared to drive a single pair of stones by one-step gearing. To the waterwheel shaft was attached a large face gear which was engaged into a lantern pinion, often called a wallower. The purpose of the gears was twofold: to transfer the direction of the drive from horizontal to vertical, and to increase the speed of the millstone spindle as opposed to the slower motion of the waterwheel shaft. The ratio of the gears varied according to the individual ideas of millwrights, but was often around 1:5. A good millwright avoided simple gear ratios by the insertion of a "hunting cog" (e.g., there might be 61 cogs in the face wheel and 10 in the lantern pinion). This precaution ensured that the same two cogs did not continuously mesh together in a regular pattern, thus avoiding potential uneven wear due to inequalities in the repeatedly meeting cog-faces.

Most of the face-gear wheels in the early mills were constructed with two wooden arms passing through mortices in the waterwheel shaft to form four spokes. The rims, which were pegged or bolted to the arms, were laminated, the two thicknesses being pinned together with bolts or treenails and arranged so that the grain of the wood crossed at right angles. Each ring of the rim was in four segments known as "cants." The joints of the cants were staggered so that they came together directly in the center of the cant in the adjoining ring. The cogs were driven into mortices in the sides or faces of the cants, passed through both thicknesses, and were secured in place by pegs or wedges in the shank ends.

Lantern pinions were built of solid wood discs at top and bottom connected by a ring of wooden staves, which were set

DRAWING OF THE UPPER MILLS, A RECONSTRUCTED LATE
SEVENTEENTH CENTURY WATER MILL,
AT PHILIPSBURG MANOR, NORTH TARRYTOWN, NEW YORK.

The water to power the mill is conducted from the mill
pond to the water wheel by the flume [1], a large wooden
trough. The amount of water fed to the wheel is controlled
by the flume gate [2], which is lifted or lowered by a series
of levers attached to a block-and-tackle arrangement inside
the mill building. This also provides the start-and-stop
arrangement for the mill machinery. When the flume gate
is lifted, the water emerges under pressure from the base
of the flume and strikes the buckets [3] of the water wheel,
causing it to revolve. After powering the wheel, the water
flows away down the tail race [4].

The arms, or spokes, of the water wheel are morticed into
the main shaft [5], which is the solid trunk of a white oak
tree, and which in its present form is 25 feet 9 inches long
and 22 inches in diameter. The oak shaft transmits the
power into the mill building where, on the stone floor [6],
there are two pairs of 54-inch French Burr millstones.
Attached to the main shaft are two face gear wheels [7],
one directly under each pair of stones. The face gear
wheels engage into lantern pinions [8], which are mounted
on the millstone spindles [9], thus transferring the drive
from horizontal to vertical. The gearing also increases the
shaft speed; the actual ratio is 3 to 14, with 56 gear teeth
[10] in the face gear wheel and only 12 teeth, or staves, in
the lantern pinion.

The millstone spindles pass through a wooden bearing,
called the neck bearing [11], in the center of the bedstone,
above which they protrude about 8 inches. The runner
stone [12] is pivoted on top of the spindle by a small socket
bearing called the cock eye in the center of the rynd [13], a
bowed iron crossbar. The pivot point of the spindle is
known as the cock head which fits into the cock eye. Just
above the neck bearing on a square section of the spindle is

fitted the driver [14], a piece of cast iron, which turns the
runner stone by engaging into recesses on either side of the
eye. Thus the runner stone revolves and the bedstone [15]
is stationary.

The millstone spindles are supported by foot-step bearings
fitted into bridging boxes mounted on the bridgetree [16],
which can be raised or lowered. This process is known as
tentering and controls the space between the stones by
lifting or lowering the runner stone by the spindle, thus
producing finer or coarser meal as required. (In the
drawing it was not possible to show the actual tentering
staffs, which raise or lower the bridgetree.)

To the right of the millstones is shown the stone crane [17],
used to turn the runner stone over for dressing, or
sharpening.

The windlass barrel [18] for the sack hoist is driven by a
further lantern pinion [19] from one of the face gear wheels
so as to give a right-angled, horizontal drive.

When required for grinding, the grain is tipped into the
grain bins [20] on the grain floor [21]. From the bins the
grain flows by gravitation into a spout which delivers it into
the hopper [22], supported by the horse [23], which rests
on top of the round wooden case, called the vat [24]. The
base of the hopper feeds the grain into the shoe [25], an
inclined tapering wooden trough. The shoe is hung free at
its top end from the horse and held in position at its lower
end by leather straps and a wooden spring. As the runner
millstone revolves it also turns the damsel [26], a 2-inch
square wooden shaft, which projects upwards to a bearing
in the horse. As the damsel rotates, its corners tap against a
block of wood in the shoe which causes it to vibrate and
shake a steady stream of grain into the eye [27], the center
hole in the runner stone. The chatter of the damsel makes
it the noisiest piece of equipment in the mill, and this is
why it is so named.

The amount of grain being fed into the millstones is
regulated by a slide in the base of the hopper which is

adjusted by the handle which, in the drawing, protrudes just above the left-hand side of the hopper. A further adjustment to the grain feed is made by raising or lowering the lower end of the shoe by means of the leather strap which is attached to the twist peg on the top left-hand corner of the horse.

From the shoe the grain falls into the eye of the runner stone, passes between the stones and emerges as meal all around the periphery of the stones and is trapped in the vat. The revolving upper stone carries the meal around to the meal spout [28], where it is discharged into the meal trough [29] on the meal floor [30], where it is put into sacks or barrels for delivery or for bolting, which is a sifting process.

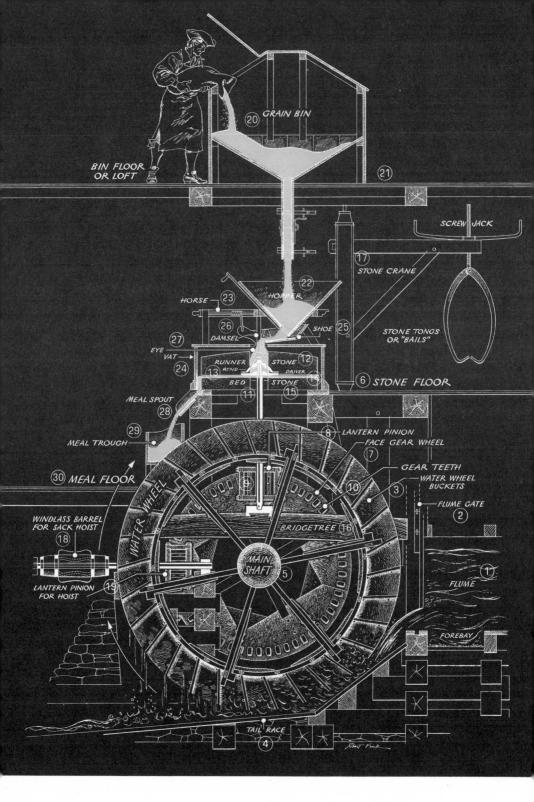

BIN FLOOR OR LOFT

GRAIN BIN ⑳

㉑

SCREW JACK

⑰ STONE CRANE

HORSE ㉓

HOPPER

㉒

STONE TONGS OR "BAILS"

㉖ DAMSEL

SHOE

㉕

EYE ㉗
VAT
㉔

RUNNER STONE ⑫
RYND
⑬ STONE DRIVER

⑥ STONE FLOOR

BED STONE
⑪ ⑮

MEAL SPOUT
㉘

⑧ LANTERN PINION

FACE GEAR WHEEL
⑦

MEAL TROUGH ㉙

GEAR TEETH

⑳ MEAL FLOOR

WATER WHEEL BUCKETS

⑨

⑩

③

FLUME GATE
②

WINDLASS BARREL FOR SACK HOIST

⑱

BRIDGETREE ⑯

MAIN SHAFT
⑤

①

LANTERN PINION FOR HOIST
⑲

FLUME

FOREBAY

TAIL RACE
④

into them and served as cogs. The lantern pinions were mounted on the millstone spindles that passed through a wooden bearing, called the "neck" bearing, in the center of the stationary lower stone or bedstone. To provide lubrication for the neck bearing there were usually recesses in the contact surface which were packed with grease-soaked wool.

In the early colonial mills the upper millstone, the runner stone, was attached to the spindle by a "stiff rynd," which engaged into the stone by fitting into recesses around the eye. The rynd was usually of cast iron in the form of a cross or a curved cross. The arms of the cross were called "claws," and the usual type of rynd was called a four-clawed rynd. A few installations had three-armed rynds, known as three-clawed rynds. In later mills the eye of the runner stone was fitted with a "balance rynd," or "millstone bridge," a thick curved iron bar which crossed the eye and fitted into slots sunk about ¾ inch into the stone. Frequently two such crosspieces of iron were placed at right angles to each other, with the ends of balance rynds secured to the stone by lead run into the slots. In the center of the balance rynds was a socket called a "cock eye," the supporting bearing for the runner stone. The pivot point of the millstone spindle, known as the "cock head," fitted into the cock eye. Where the balance rynd was formed of two crosspieces, the ends of one of these pieces would be sunk about 2½ inches deeper into the stone than the ends of the other piece, to allow for the recesses in the stone to accommodate the "driver." This was a heavy piece of cast iron which fitted on the spindle to connect the drive to the stone. Runner stones fitted with balance rynds were much easier to balance than those fitted on stiff rynds, because the stone could swing freely on the cock head and adjust itself to the bedstone. In the case of the stiff rynd, the weight of the runner stone was supported by the ends of the claws at three or four points and was not free to swing. To balance stones pivoted on a cock head, lead was run into crevices in the top of the stone on its lightest side. The millstone spindles were supported by foot-step bearings fitted into bridging boxes mounted on bridge-trees that could be raised or lowered. This process was known as "tentering," and controlled the clearance between the stones, thus producing finer or coarser meal as required.

As the American colonies expanded and the population increased, higher production was required from the mills. To satisfy this increased demand, many mills were enlarged and larger and more powerful waterwheels were installed. Gearing systems were adapted so that more than one pair of stones could be driven from a single waterwheel. Some waterwheel shafts were simply made longer so as to accommodate two face-gear wheels, each of which would drive a pair or run of stones; in other installations the two-step gear train was developed, usually in one of two patterns. In one system a larger and more strongly constructed face gear was mounted on the waterwheel shaft. This larger gear wheel had more arms and cants than the face wheels fitted in the earlier mills and was known as the "big face wheel" or "master face wheel." The big face wheel drove one or two lantern pinions or wallowers on lay-shafts set at right angles. On the wallower shafts were "little face wheels," which meshed into lantern pinions, often called "trundles," on the millstone spindles. The wallower gudgeon nearest the main shaft rested in a sliding block so that either wallower could be disengaged by the use of a lever. This gearing system was referred to as "counter gears."

In the other two-step gearing arrangement, a large face gear was mounted on the waterwheel shaft. In this case the gear wheel was usually called the "pit wheel" because the bottom half ran in a pit. The pit wheel meshed into a lantern wallower attached to a sturdy wooden upright known as the upright shaft. Higher up on the upright shaft, often just above the wallower, was mounted a large spur gear wheel, usually called the "great spur wheel," in which the cogs or teeth were driven into mortices in the edge of the rim. The cogs of the great spur wheel meshed into lantern or spur pinions attached to the millstone spindles. This arrangement was called "spur gear drive." Spur gear drive usually came from below the millstones and was known as underdrift, but in isolated cases the spur wheel was positioned above the millstones so that the drive came downward and was known as overdrift. Overdrift was the more usual method used in windmills that were equipped with spur wheel drive. Several pairs of millstones could be arranged around a spur wheel according to its size, but usually there were two to four pairs.

Although in some instances two-step gearing was developed so that additional millstones could be driven from a single waterwheel, two-step gearing also became necessary when waterwheels were built of a larger diameter so that millstones could be operated at an efficient speed. The speed of the shaft of a waterwheel of larger diameter was, of course, slower than that of a smaller waterwheel. Because it was not practicable to build up the required speed by one-step gearing, the two-step gearing system was adopted.

The millstones were the heart of a colonial grist- or flour-mill. In early colonial days many of the stones used were imported from England and Germany. Those from England were quarried in southwest Yorkshire and the northeastern perimeter of Derbyshire. The millstones cut from this rock, appropriately known as Millstone Grit, were referred to by British millers as "Peak" or "Grey" stones.

The millstones from Germany were quarried at Neider Menting in the Mayen district of the Rhineland. This stone was a dark bluish grey lava with even pores, known to millers as "Cullin" stones. Cullin is an approximation of Köln, the German name of Cologne, the city through which these stones were shipped down the Rhine from Andernach. Cullin stones were also called Holland stones, Blue stones, Rhine stones, and Cologne stones. These millstones were very popular with the Dutch settlers; and Cullin millstones or pieces of them can be seen at many Dutch colonial mill sites.

Many sources of native rock were used to produce millstones in colonial America. In New York State the best-known millstone quarries were in an area known as the Traps, near High Falls in Ulster County. The stones from this area were called Esopus millstones and were cut from deposits of

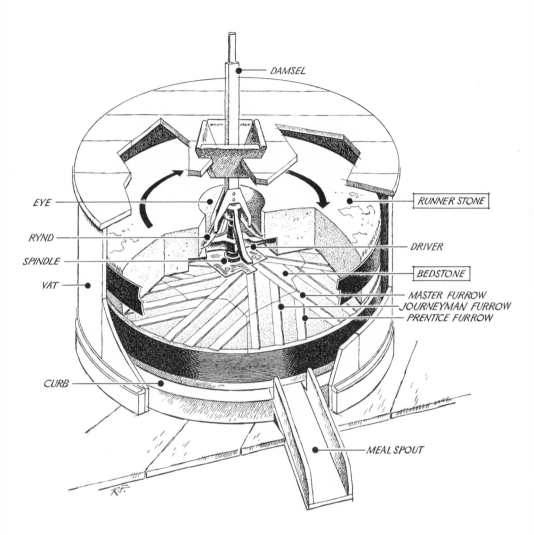

DAMSEL

EYE

RYND

SPINDLE

VAT

CURB

RUNNER STONE

DRIVER

BEDSTONE

MASTER FURROW
JOURNEYMAN FURROW
PRENTICE FURROW

MEAL SPOUT

This cutaway drawing shows the grinding action of the two millstones with a right-hand dress.

Shawangunk Conglomerate Grit. In Connecticut, quartz-shot sandstone was quarried from Mount Tom to produce millstones for the early settlements in that area and for many of the mills on Long Island. The granite from the well-known quarries at Westerly, Rhode Island, and quarries in New Hampshire provided many of the stones used in New England mills. In Pennsylvania there were millstone quarries in Lancaster County, Berkshire County, and Bowmanstown in Carbon County. Quarries were also worked to produce millstones in Virginia and a quartz-bearing granite was used for millstones from quarries in Rowan County, North Carolina. In fact, there were probably millstone quarries in most areas where there was a suitable hard stone and where grain milling was carried on to any extent. The size of these native millstones varied from less than 2 up to 7 feet in diameter. When new, these stones would vary from about 8 to 30 inches in thickness, and the largest stones would weigh more than 3,500 pounds.

From quite early in the eighteenth century millstones built up of blocks of a French stone began to be imported. At first most of these French millstones came complete from English millstone makers. Later the blocks of stone were imported to America and assembled into complete millstones in this country. This French stone was the best and most popular stone ever discovered for grinding wheat into white flour. The stone was a freshwater quartz quarried at La Ferté-sous-Jouarre near the town of Châlons in the Marne Valley in Northern France, and found only in small pieces ranging from about 12 to 18 inches long, from 6 to 10 inches wide, by 5 to 10 inches thick, usually embedded in layers of clay. Very infrequently a piece of stone would be quarried large enough to make a millstone in one piece: but usually a French millstone of popular size— 4 feet to 4 feet 6 inches—had to be built from pieces, or "burrs" as they were usually termed. French Burr (or buhr) stones produced a whiter flour from wheat because the extremely hard surface of the stone was far less abrasive than any other stone used. An abrasive stone tended to shred the outer part of the grain of wheat, the bran, into a powder. This

The sections of a complete stone and the "dress," or layout of the furrows, in a French buhr millstone, from Philipsburg Manor, Upper Mills, North Tarrytown, New York. Photo: Erich Hartmann/Magnum.

fine powdered bran dressed through the bolting cloth of the flour-dressing machinery or bolters, together with the white part of the wheat meal; and the flour thus produced was of a darker color. By the 1750s French Burr stones had become very popular with colonial millers, particularly those engaged in the export business. The use of French stones enabled them to produce flour of quality comparable to that produced by European mills.

Another reason for the superiority of French stones was their high porosity. Some pieces were simply a mass of porous cells; as the stones wore away, new cutting edges appeared. Because they could be worked for a long time without being refaced or redressed, they were very popular with millers. Some remained in normal use a century or more.

The process of building the complete millstones from the blocks of rough French stone began with selecting suitable pieces, usually to form two concentric rings looking rather like keystones of an arch. The number of sectional pieces used varied, depending on the size of the blocks; some French millstones had more than 20 sections. The sections of stone were trimmed and dressed to fit and form a perfectly round solid millstone. As in the case of all millstones, the runner had a round hole in the center, usually about 10 inches in diameter, to form the eye, through which the grain was fed. The bedstone was built with a square hole in the center about 10 inches across to accommodate the neck bearing of the driving or balancing spindle. The pieces of stone were cemented or plastered together and bound with iron bands to prevent bursting when the millstones were in use. These bands were usually "sweated" or shrunk on, that is, the iron bands were heated red-hot and thus would expand. In this red-hot condition the bands were driven over the edge of the stones; as the bands cooled, they contracted and became extremely tight. The top of the French runner stone was usually finished off with a layer of plaster of Paris to form a slightly convex top. When new, a French runner stone of 4 feet to 4 feet 6 inches in diameter was usually about 12 to 15 inches thick at the circumference, known as the "skirt" of the millstone, and 15 to 18 inches thick at the eye or center. These runner stones weighed more than 2,400 pounds.

The under side of the French bedstone was smoothed off to a perfectly level finish with a layer of plaster of Paris, so that the stone would lie flat on its base. To correct any uneven spots, all bedstones, of whatever type of stone, were leveled by driving wooden wedges under the stone in the appropriate spots. The lower surface of the runner stones and the upper surface of the bedstones were grooved, or "furrowed," in a pattern which caused the meal to flow away from the centers of the stones to their circumferences. The layout of the furrows was referred to as the "dress," which generally followed one of two patterns— the "sickle" dress or the "quarter" dress.

Many millstones used in early colonial mills were dressed with the "sickle" or circular furrow dress. This arrangement of furrows was usually marked out on the stones by using the same radius as in the size of the stones, for example, a 4 foot stone had a 2 foot radius. To mark out a left-hand pair of stones, that is, a pair of stones in which the runner revolved counterclockwise, the base point of the compass would be set in the periphery of the stone to the left of the stone eye, with the marker point away from the person using the compass. For a right-hand millstone, the same procedure would be carried out, working, of course, to the right-hand side of the eye. There was a great variation in the number of furrows used, some stones having more than 100, while there were others with as few as four. The sickle furrows were usually narrow at the eye and broadened out as they reached the skirt. This spread was as much as from ½ inch at the eye to 2 inches at the skirt, or on larger stones perhaps even more.

The word "quarter" when applied to millstones does not mean a fourth part of the area of the stone, but refers to the number of the sections containing the furrows. The quarters were determined by the master furrows. The leading edge of these furrows did not radiate from the dead center of the eye to the skirt but ran tangentially to an imaginary circle around the center of the eye. In a stone which revolved counterclockwise, they were tangent to the left-hand of the center of the eye; if the stones revolved clockwise, they were tangent to the right-hand of the center of the eye. The circle was called a draft circle, and its radius was known as the draft. For example, stones with a 6-inch draft circle would have a 3-inch draft. The larger the draft, the more quickly was the ground material carried to the skirt of the stone. Usually there was a smaller draft on stones used mainly for grinding wheat flour, larger drafts being found on stones used mainly for coarser grinding, as in the case of animal feeds.

Running parallel to the master furrows were secondary furrows. In some cases these furrows would be cut so as to join with the next master furrow, while on other millstones they would terminate just short of the adjoining master furrow. There were many combinations to form the quarters; a millstone might be marked out with 20 quarters of two furrows, nine quarters of six, 16 quarters of three; in fact, these combinations were many and various and depended on the individual ideas of the millwright or miller. A popular dress was nine quarters of four furrows. These four furrows were termed by millers as: the "master furrow," the second the "journeyman furrow," the third the "prentice," and the fourth, the shortest, the "butterfly furrow." A millstone dressed with combinations of three furrows had no "fly furrow," and any combinations of two furrows had master and journeyman only. In different areas, of course, different terms might be used for the shorter furrows.

Regardless of the type of dress, the leading edges of the furrows were usually vertical and from ¼ to ¾ inch in depth, this depth gradually tapering off to come up to the grinding surface of the stone. The width of furrows in a millstone with quarter dress was usually between 1 inch and 1¼ inches. The grinding edge at the top of the tapering furrow was known to millers as the "feather edge," and millstones ground feather edge to feather edge.

The furrows were laid out in exactly the same way on both

Charles Howell dressing a millstone with a mill bill.

stones, so that, when the runner was turned over for dressing, the design on the grinding faces of both stones was identical. When a pair of millstones were in working position, with the two grinding faces together, as the runner stone revolved the furrows crossed each other to create a positive shearing action, rather like many pairs of scissors in action.

The areas between the furrows, usually about 10 inches from the circumference of the stones, was known as "lands." The lands were dressed with fine lines called "cracks." In a French stone used solely for grinding wheat flour, it was the practice of experienced stonemen to insert about 16 cracks to the inch, depending on the texture of the stone. In millstones used for grinding corn or animal feed, the cracks varied from three to six per inch, again, depending on the ideas of individual millers. The area around the eye of the stones was "faced" off so that when the lands were almost in contact, this area would be slightly further apart. This relief permitted the grain to enter between the stones for preliminary breaking prior to being ground finer at the skirt of the stones.

To turn the runner stone over for dressing, a heavy wooden crane was used. This was fitted with a large pair of iron tongs, or "bails," the ends of which fitted into holes drilled on opposite sides of the stone to receive them. Sometimes the ends of the tongs were holed so that loose pins were secured into the tong holes and thence into the corresponding holes in the stone. The tongs were fitted with a screwjack, which in the early days was often of hardwood and later of wrought iron. The tongs were wide enough to permit the stone to be turned over before being lowered on its back, so that the grinding face could be dressed. The cranes could be swung to one side when not in use. Sometimes the "runner" was turned over by pulley blocks or other devices.

The tools used for dressing or sharpening the grinding faces of the millstones were "mill bills," "mill picks," or "millpecks." The mill bills were usually shaped like a double-ended wedge and made from steel which had been tempered so the chisel-like edges would cut the stone. Mill bills were about 7 to 9 inches long and had a hole in the thick center part into which wooden handles were fitted, so the bills could be used somewhat like a hammer.

Sometimes the mill bills were fitted into a "bill-thrift" made of a turned wooden handle about 12 to 15 inches in length and shaped almost like a mallet. The thick end was about 3 inches in diameter, with a mortice cut to accommodate the bill. The mill "picks" or "pecks" were sometimes so named to distinguish them from the chisel-ended bills, because some of these tools were pointed at the ends in order to "peck" holes in the surface of the stones. However, they were used in exactly the same way as the bills. When using these millstone dressing tools, the dresser would usually half-recline over a cushion or "bist" made from a part sack of meal or bran. The bist also steadied the hands of the dresser so the lines or cracks could be cut reasonably straight in the stone. Stone dressing was a tedious job: it took a good workman about 14 hours to dress each stone.

Millers argued about the relative efficiency of the various dresses used on the stones and the quantity of grain which could be ground between dressings. However, these measures depended on the fineness of the grind; because the finer the meal, the more often the stones needed dressing. It seems, however, that an average of about 50 tons could be ground on a pair of stones before redressing was required.

Stone case, tun, vat, hoop, and husk were the names applied to the wooden casings around the millstones, which were often made from a soft wood such as white pine or poplar. The casings were made 2 to 4 inches wider than the diameter of the millstones. Some runner stones were fitted with a tag known as a "sweeper"; as the stone revolved, this tag would sweep between the edge of the stones and the case and thus carry the meal to the spout opening. In many instances, however, the meal was carried to the spout by the movement of the revolving stone.

On top of the stone case was fitted the "horse" or "hopper ladder," made of wood and usually with four legs that fitted into slots in the case. The horse held the hopper in position; and at the base of the hopper was fitted a slide which controlled the amount of grain that was fed into the "shoe." A reciprocating movement was conveyed to the shoe by a "damsel." The damsel was usually a short square shaft of wood attached to the top of the center of the rynd in the eye of the runner stone so that, as the stone turned, the damsel revolved with it. The corners of the damsel tapped against a block on the inside of the shoe, causing it to vibrate and feed an even trickle of grain into the eye of the stone. The chatter of the damsel made it the noisiest piece of equipment in the mill and earned it its name. In later mills the damsels were frequently made of iron. After the grain had passed between the stones, it passed down a spout to a lower floor or level, the spout usually discharging into a wooden trough for cooling purposes. From the trough it was scooped or shoveled into barrels or sacks.

In the early small mills, the grain was tipped directly into the millstone hoppers from the sacks or barrels. The larger and later mills had bins (or garners) positioned on an upper floor above the millstone hoppers. From the bins the grain was gravity fed through a spout into the hoppers. Many upper mill floors were arranged so that damp grain could be spread out for drying purposes before being put into the bins. The grain floors and bins also provided valuable storage space for the grain prior to grinding.

When colonial watermills were first established, the water-wheel provided power for little else apart from the millstones, the exception being perhaps a sack hoist. Some of these hoists were operated by a lantern pinion which engaged the cogs of a face gear at horizontal right angles. The lantern pinion was attached to a windlass barrel which turned continuously as the mill was in operation. A rope would have two slack turns around the barrel; the other end of the rope would be over a pulley, probably in a beam which projected from the gable end of the roof just above a doorway, so that the rope with a hook on its end would be outside the end of the building. To lift barrels or sacks into the top floor of the mill from carts, or perhaps boats, the hook would be attached to a barrel or sack. Then the person outside would signal to the men inside the mill to tighten the rope around the revolving windlass barrel. Thus the rope would be pulled upward outside and would lift its load to the top of the mill. Sack hoists eventually became quite elaborate, with wooden friction clutches, or slack leather belt mechanisms, which permitted engaging or disengaging by control ropes from the point where the sacks were taken into the mill.

In the early days many small custom mills lacked facilities for cleaning the wheat or other grain prior to grinding. Any grain cleaning was performed by hand using sieves or screens and fans. However, as the mills became larger, and millers became merchants, waterpower was used to turn slowly revolving cylindrical wire screens through which a blast of air passed. The chaff and dust were removed by the air current and some of the other impurities were removed by the friction of the screen. The air current was usually provided by flat wooden bladed fans enclosed in a drum and driven from the mill mechanism. These power-driven fans looked almost like a very small undershot waterwheel fitted with flat boards for buckets.

As in the case of grain cleaning, the sifting of wheat meal to produce a finer flour was at first done by hand, a process called bolting. In early days bolting was frequently done after the meal had left the mill in homes, in bakeshops, and in some cases in bolting houses set up especially for the purpose.

The sieves used were first made of woven wire, then of horsehair, wool yarn, and linen. The best-equipped mills at the end of the colonial period used silk for bolting cloth. From the simple hand sieves many varied hand-turned bolting machines developed. Some bolting machines were rectangular inclined sieves mounted in a frame, one end of which supported a hopper. From the hopper the meal flowed onto the sieve which usually had finer bolting cloth at its top section and coarser cloth in the lower section. The finest flour dropped through the top section, the coarser through the lower part, and the bran and middlings went over the end of the sieve. The sieve was vibrated by a square shaft of wood on which the upper end of the sieve rested, while the shaft was rotated by a handle. The incline of the sieve was adjustable on its supports at the lower end.

Another type of bolting machine consisted of cylindrical, square, or polygonal reels, which in the early days were about 6 feet long and possibly 2 feet in diameter. Flour-dressing reels had a central wooden shaft from which short spokes radiated, with wooden slats laid lengthwise on the outer edge of the spokes. These slats had rounded edges and were closer together in the case of a cylindrical reel; in the case of polygonal reels, there would be as many lengthwise slats as there were sides. For example, there would be six lengthwise slats for a hexagonal reel, but only four for a square one.

This light wooden framework was covered with bolting cloth of three different degrees of fineness. The finest was at the head end of the reel and the coarsest at the foot or tail end. The reel was tilted slightly; at the head end it was higher than at the foot. As the reel was slowly revolved, the wheat meal was fed in at the head end. The finest particles went throught the fine-meshed cloth at the head section. Through the center section of the reel, which was covered with a coarser cloth, went some of the material left over from the first section of the reel and some larger particles making up the middlings. The product going through the coarsest cloth nearest the foot was called "sharps" or "shorts." The remaining coarse particles or bran passed out of the reel at its lower end. Square or polygonal reels gave a more positive sifting process because of the tumbling action created by the revolving flat sides. Under the varying meshed sections of the reels were placed wooden dividers to guide the different grades to spouts that filled sacks or barrels positioned below.

After about 1730 most mills of any size drove the flour bolters by waterpower. Many different systems of transmitting the power to these machines were utilized, such as various types of light wooden gearing and wooden shafting, which had pulleys connected by rope or flat leather belt drives. Many mills had inclined rectangular sieves placed under meal spouts which received their reciprocating motion from a connecting rod activated by a simple wooden cam on the head of a lantern pinion or a cam attached to the millstone spindle. These simple types of sieves were often used for corn meal or buckwheat flour, and covered with cloth or wire woven in meshes of various sizes. Toward the end of the colonial period, the large merchant mills had quite elaborate systems of bolting. The cylindrical or polygonal reels were much larger, perhaps over 20 feet in length and 30 inches in diameter. Some mills would have several reels enclosed in wooden cabinets, so that the flour would not be blown around the mill. In many of these large later mills, the middlings were often returned to the millstones for further grinding and then fed back on to the reels for additional sifting.

During the colonial period water-driven grist- and flourmills progressed from the primitive horizontal mills housed in tiny log cabins to the large commercial or "merchant" mills with substantial stone buildings, some of which were up to six stories in height. The products of the mills had improved from the coarse brown wholewheat meal to superfine white flour, and the production capacities increased from a few pounds an hour to perhaps more than 3,000 pounds an hour.

In remote country districts many of the mills remained small and ground grain only to satisfy the needs of local inhabitants. This grinding was done on a "custom" basis; with the miller usually keeping a percentage of the meal, called "miller's toll," for payment. The toll varied, but was often 15 to 20 percent. The output of many of these mills was quite small, perhaps little more than three or four bushels per hour. These became known as "custom mills."

In time some of the large "merchant mills" grew into quite prosperous and important business enterprises. The wheat was bought in large quantities from farmers and milled into flour, which was then sold, much of it for export. Large and powerful waterwheels drove these merchant mills, some of which had six or more pairs of millstones. They were equipped

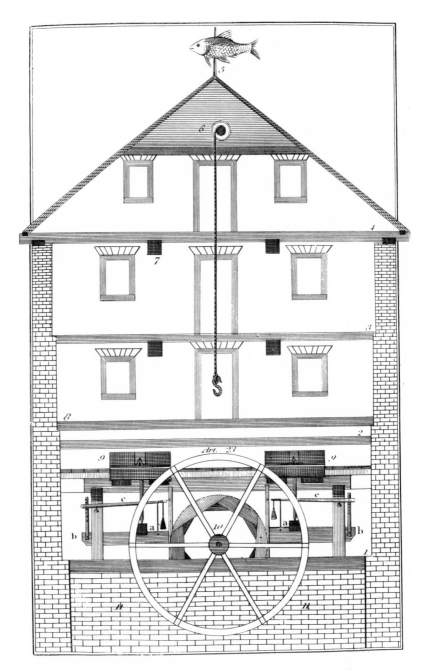

A layout of a commercial mill (Oliver Evans).

with quite efficient machinery for cleaning the grain, and the improved silken-cloth bolters produced flour of excellent quality. Most of the flour, particularly that intended for export, was packed in barrels. Daily production from the mills was measured in barrels, a standard barrel of flour being 196 pounds. Besides providing work for millers, these merchant mills needed the services of many coopers to make and repair the large number of barrels used.

Apart from a powerful waterpower site, good transportation —by water or road—was essential to the successful operation of merchant mills. Mills on or near navigable rivers were most valuable, particularly when they were situated near good wheat growing areas. Navigation could bring cargoes of wheat to the mill and take loads of flour to ports and other markets.

From the start, the availability of timber, as we have seen, was a key factor in the development of waterpower and watermills. The extensive use of wood recurs at each phase of the milling operation, from housing and construction of the mills themselves to the packing of the final product for foreign export.

Waterpower in the Century of the Steam Engine

Louis C. Hunter

THE ROLE of steam power in early industrialization has been exaggerated and the reasons for its preeminence misunderstood. The traditional explanation for its rise to preeminence—mobility, flexibility in capacity, and all-seasons reliability—are projections of later experience upon the past and have limited relevance in many situations.

The common view, at best an oversimplification, rests upon two misleading assumptions. One presents British experience as the model on which industrialization proceeded, in the use of motive power as well as in other essentials such as the shift from hand to machine operations, concentration in factories, division of labor, and the like. The other assumption, also more commonly implied than expressed, views the steam engine as intrinsically superior to water as a source of motive power. Yet much of British experience with stationary power was exceptional rather than typical, and thus in particularly striking contrast to the course of American industrial development prior to the 1860s. American industry rested largely—before the 1840s, overwhelmingly—upon waterpower, a fact partially obscured by the glamour surrounding the historic role assigned Watt in the Industrial Revolution. In the background, too, is the lingering view that associates waterpower with obsolescence, if not backwardness. Some writers have minimized American "backwardness," focusing on those areas of mechanization in which Americans applied steampower with early and striking success, namely steam navigation on inland and coastal waters and, somewhat later, railways. Except for the obligatory reference to New England, especially the city of Lowell, where waterpower was redeemed by the scale on which it was used, this source of motive power is rarely stressed.

Some historians of industry and technology have contributed to this confusion by repeating the account of Britain's early development and primary reliance upon the steam engine, as pioneered by Newcomen and Watt. Watt invented; Boulton & Watt built; and Victorian England celebrated the prime mover that, with global repercussions, was shortly to place hundreds of thousands of mechanical slaves at the disposal of British industry. Watt was assigned the role of "father of the steam engine," a status almost without challenge for at least a century. In the words of an early English engineer-historian, Watt had "done more for art and commerce than any single individual ever known."[1] A generation later a leading American technologist declared in even loftier language, "On this planet man is the noblest work of God and the evolution of steam power is the noblest work of men."[2]

Waterpower in its time has not been without its celebrants; and historians have described the evolution of its central component, the waterwheel, from the first evidences of its possible use in classical times down through the Middle Ages and later. They have traced the widening range of its applications from the elevation of water for irrigation and other uses, especially in the eastern Mediterranean basins, and the grinding of bread-grains, long the widest and most important of its preindustrial uses, to mining, metalworking, and a variety of forms of milling.[3] A reasonably clear, if still incomplete, picture is available of the extension of waterpower through the Western world. With the coming of the Industrial Revolution, however, the scene and central character quickly change, in technological as in human affairs, the forces of upheaval are ruthless in the elevation of new gods to replace the old. Historians hitched their wagons to the rising star of steam; and waterpower, wheels and all, passed into the limbo of irrelevance, there to await the second coming effected by the electrical transmission of power.

The Victorian view of the revolutionary role of steampower, not without its measure of validity, has been accepted by historians almost without challenge. This has been especially true of those broad-gauge interpretations so influential with the general audience, in which the subtler shades of interpretation are avoided for the sake of brevity. In its treatment of the Industrial Revolution a well-known single-volume survey of the history of technology dismisses waterpower, except for some incidental references, with a single page at the opening of a long chapter on the steam engine.[4] A more recent and somewhat more comprehensive interpretation of technology in Western civilization opens a chapter on "The Prerequisites of Industrialization" (which makes no reference to water-wheels) with the statement: "When we think of the Industrial Revolution we usually think of the steam engine, the railway locomotive and the factory system . . ." Precisely! More than a century earlier, Marx and Engels in their *Communist Manifesto* had given wide currency to the concept in declaring that "steam and machinery revolutionized industrial production."[5]

There is, of course, no challenging the generally accepted view that the nineteenth was indeed the century of the steam engine. The century may be said to have been launched, symbolically as well as literally, in 1800, the year in which the basic patent of Watt expired and the celebrated Boulton & Watt partnership was terminated. By this date the low-pressure, condensing stationary engine in its basic pumping and rotative forms was securely established in practical use, and the field of steam engineering opened legitimately to all comers. The century ended, somewhat ahead of schedule, in the 1890s when the steam turbine in the several forms pioneered by de Laval, Parsons, and others, moved ahead toward its swift triumph. By 1914 the steam turbine, paired typically on land with the electric dynamo, had made the classic reciprocating-piston engine obsolete. The steam engine as employed in mine, mill, and factory, with which this discussion is concerned, was, of course, but one of the three segments constituting the steampower base of industrialization. Steampower in its mobile applications, railway locomotives and steam vessels, had an aggregate impact no less significant than stationary steam power.[6] Without steampowered transportation the advance of industrialization would have been greatly retarded, since increased production depended on access to markets and raw materials and on rapid communications. The eventual "victory" of steampower in transportation over the traditional natural sources of motive power—stream flow and the winds—was decisive. Stream flow offered but a passing competition to steam navigation: what it gave in downstream flatboat and barge traffic was largely offset by the heavy handicap, virtually an embargo, imposed on upstream commerce. But the massive and progressively efficient application of windpower in marine commerce did delay the takeover by steam vessels until the closing decades of the nineteenth century.[7]

There is, however, no evidence that steampower is intrinsically superior to waterpower in its operation of driven machinery. Characteristics of supply have no bearing on the functioning of engine and waterwheel. Assuming that the fuel and water supply required by the steam engine and the water flow of a given volume and head required by the waterwheel are available, the energy delivered on the wheel shaft in each case is identical in character. Maintaining regularity of motion is quite another matter. Steam engines and waterwheels of different types each presented somewhat distinctive problems and conditions.[8]

In Britain, the key role of steampower was almost as much the result of geography as of human management. Even in the mining industries, to whose service steampower was almost entirely applied for nearly 100 years, the facts of geography were largely compelling. Mines and waterpower were almost equally unmovable. Mines, unlike mills, could not be taken to waterpower sites; and transmission distances from the latter by the available means—rods, ropes, and contour-course headraces—were typically measured in hundreds of yards, cumbrous in operation, and low in efficiency.[9] The basic geographic condition that turned Britain inescapably to steampower, especially at the higher levels of industry, was its very limited area. Rivers, though numerous, were necessarily short, drainage (catchment) basins, with a volume of stream flow typically very limited in a land so small that few points were more than a vigorous day's walk from tidewater.[10] There was no lack of waterpower of sufficient capacity to meet what, before the beginnings of industrialization, was its principal use: the grinding of bread grains. About 6,000 mills were reported by the eleventh-century inquest of Domesday, serving an estimated population of two million and distributed widely through the south and east of England.[11] In time, even the supply of small waterpowers gave out, and windmills multiplied greatly; except in the fen country where extensively employed in land drainage, they too were chiefly "corn-mills." A correspondent of Oliver Evans, visiting England in 1793, reported that there was "hardly a piece of high ground in England but is covered with them" and even in the valleys they were so thick that in many a spot one could count more than 30.[12] Rex Wailes has estimated the entire number, in 1820, at about 5,000.[13]

England's longest and greatest river, the Thames, above London, was only 200 miles long. Such major rivers as the Severn, Trent, and Great Ouse ranged from 160 to 210 miles. The entire length of the Mersey, including its estuary, was only 70 miles; the Clyde, described as "the only great British river, besides the Severn, flowing west," and "the most important river in Scotland," was, by its windings to Glasgow, 75 miles long.[14] The absence of any comprehensive survey of water resources in the British Isles as late as 1937, and the incomplete census data on motive power leaves the aggregate supply of waterpower, used and potential, in doubt.[15] That it was comparatively small is suggested by *The Final Report on the Fourth Census of Production* (1930), which stated that waterpower then constituted but 1.4 percent of the total industrial and central-station power in use in the United Kingdom.[16]

The deficiencies in British waterpower resources were particularly striking in the larger capacities. With industrial growth fairly well advanced by the 1820s, there must have

been little alternative to steampower, other locational considerations apart, for establishments requiring 40 to 50 horsepower or more.[17] Probably the largest developed waterpower
facility in Britain at this time was the Fairbairn-designed installation at the Catrine textile mills in Ayrshire, Scotland. Together, the two great Fairbairn breastwheels developed 240
horsepower on a 48-foot fall.[18] The largest single waterpower
development in Britain as late as 1880 was the celebrated
Shaw's Water Works at Greenock, near Glasgow on the Clyde,
and in its way it is almost as widely known in the engineering
world as that at Lowell on the Merrimack, although it has but
one-sixth the capacity. Completed in the early 1830s, this
imaginative and skillfully engineered system, based on a sizable artifical reservoir in nearby hills, supplied a succession of
about 30 mills, in two rows down the steep slope leading into
Greenock. The aggregate capacity was rated at about 1,500
horsepower.[19]

For all its limitations, waterpower played a much larger role
in British industrialization than most accounts acknowledge.
Such accounts usually rely on statistical data which, derived
from inspection reports under the factory acts of 1833 and
later, and confined almost wholly to the textile industries, are
skewed toward the steampower which made its most rapid
headway in these industries. By the mid-1830s, steam accounted for two-thirds of the motive power employed in cotton
textiles, a proportion which increased steadily thereafter.[20]
Quantitative data on power for most other industries is lacking,
leading many historians to unjustified conclusions. However,
some British historians have begun to dissent from the traditional identification of industrialization with steampower. In a
recent work, Tann noted that "the important first stages of
factory development during the Industrial Revolution were
achieved largely through waterpower."[21] In a much earlier
work on the industrial development of North Wales, Dodd was
highly critical of the older writers' emphasis upon the "highly
unrepresentative" Lancashire and Yorkshire textile industries
and the resulting "legend of rapid victory for steam power and

Navigable Rivers, 1660–1700

The maps on this page and on the opposite page are from
T. S. Willan, *River Navigation in England, 1600–1750*
(New York, 1936). Reproduced by permission of
The Clarendon Press, Oxford. Only the navigable parts of
rivers are shown.

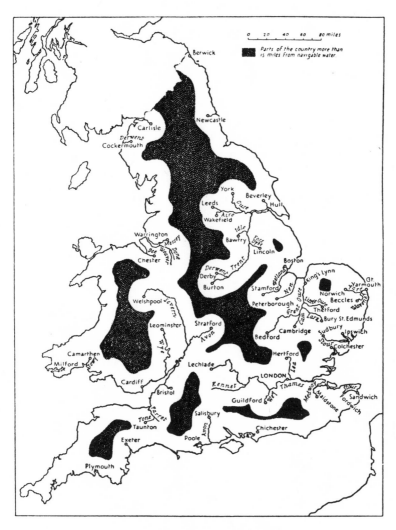

Navigable Rivers, 1724–27

big industry, accompanied by the hasty concentration of manufacturers in the coal fields."[22] In his account of the Furness district with its iron, copper, and textile industries, Marshall stressed the basic and persisting role of waterpower.[23] Hills has documented the extensive, though diminishing, reliance upon waterpower in manufacturing well into the nineteenth century.[24] How many other streams were there like the Wandle, a small tributary of the Thames, which in nine miles of its course, as surveyed in 1853, supported 38 mills with an aggregate rating of 781 horsepower, divided in number almost equally between flour mills and eight other types of manufactories![25] In her general survey, Phyllis Deane declares that "outside the textile factories and the mines, iron-works and railways, steampower was still a rarity in the mid-nineteenth century."[26]

Before turning to the American experience, let us examine another relevant aspect of Britain's development of her water resources: the manner and extent of use of rivers in transportation. From the seventeenth century, the expanding needs of inland trade and the abominable conditions, high cost, and delays of road transport led to an upsurge of river improvements. Eventually not only such main rivers as the Thames, Severn, and Trent, were brought into commercial use, but also their larger affluents and many smaller streams, interconnected by coastal waterways and, in time, with a mushrooming network of canals.[27] A century before the introduction of steam navigation in England, two-way (upstream and down) transportation by means of horse-drawn or man-propelled barges of varying but substantial capacity played a central role in domestic commerce. The extent of this system is revealed by the accompanying maps, the shaded areas showing that by 1725, much the greater part of the land was within 15 miles of navigable rivers. The use of the rivers was shared and contested by several interests. In England, the pattern of stream use and water rights, which we largely inherited with the Common Law, had its origins in Anglo-Saxon times. These several interests were reflected in such basic documents as the

Domesday Book and Magna Carta, various Royal charters and edicts and, in time, laws of Parliament. The three main parties at interest, as summarized by Thacker, are familiar enough in American experience. They were:

> . . . first, the riparian owners and the tenants of their mills and fisheries, who saw in the maintenance and increase of their weirs [dams] an easy and lucrative source of income; secondly, the bargemasters, who desired clear navigation and good floating depth for as nearly nothing as they could compass; and, lastly, the dim Riverside populations, who perpetually and sullenly complained of many things, but chiefly of the flood caused by the continual heightening of the weirs, that drove them from their homes and ruined their precarious crops; and of the wholesale, illegitimate destruction of the fry of [young] fish . . . through the illegal snares and engines commonly attached to weirs.[28]

The rights of river navigation and of river trade outlined in Magna Carta had a certain priority, but for centuries the owners of the thousands of small watermills on which the nation's bread supplies largely depended stubbornly defended their right to stream obstruction by milldams. Barge owners challenged mill owners and fishing interests, but over the years, in a manner rather different from later American experience, there developed on some of the larger streams at least an effective, if at times tenuous, symbiosis. The falls and rapids which, except during flood waters, were the bargemaster's nemesis and the miller's opportunity, were brought under control to the mutual advantage of navigation and milling, the weirs affording the increased depth of water needed by both. By the end of the eighteenth century, boat passages by means of temporary—and time- and water-wasting—openings through the dams, known as "flashes," were being replaced by the modern pound lock, a great improvement for both milling interests and barge traffic. Of the Thames, Britain's greatest river, it was reported in 1884 that "out of twenty-six pound

locks below Oxford, placed where the bargemasters most required them, and adjacent to ancient weirs, only five were
without a neighboring mill."[29]

In sum, the roots of British industrialism go deep into the
past, and waterpower played an important role in the subsistence, preindustrial, and early industrial phases of economic
development, up to the mid-nineteenth century. The record of
water resource use generally and of what was later to be termed
multiple-purpose river development was impressive. Despite
the limitations imposed by England's insular position and small
size upon her power and inland navigation potential, the effective and increasing utilization of these resources preceded the
application of steampower to navigation by a century. Yet, they
could not long delay the movement of industry to those parts of
the kingdom favored by a combination of abundant and cheap
coal, and proximity to coastal shipping facilities which afforded
access to markets and materials.

Despite a common background of British institutions, during the early decades of the nineteenth century, the United
States presented a very different situation in several important
respects. The differences reflected the newness of the country,
and the character of its natural environment and resources.
These factors created the predominant reliance of an expanding and progressive industrial base upon waterpower until the
1860s. The Federal decennial census of 1870, the first to add
motive power to such traditional categories of inquiry as capital
investment, hands employed, and value of products, revealed
steam horsepower in manufacturing leading water horsepower
in the ratio of 52 to 48, a margin which widened progressively
in succeeding decades.[30]

Before the Civil War, falling water was the principal source
of stationary power in the United States. This was true at all
levels of size and capacity in most industries, and throughout
the nation, especially in the older and more advanced industrial regions, i.e., New England and the Middle Atlantic
States. At the base of what was still, in 1860, a predominantly
agricultural economy, with an overwhelmingly rural and

small-town population, were the tens of thousands of small watermills, serving their immediate environs on a toll-exchange or limited commercial basis in such essential indus-tries as gristmilling and sawmilling. Except for the larger commercial establishments, these mills developed no more than several horsepower, and often operated intermittently or when water was available. The more specialized establish-ments, engaged in the production of cast- or forged-iron goods, wooden articles, paper, textiles (chiefly yarn), and the like, were numbered in the thousands. Typically, they served somewhat wider markets but often, to some extent at least, accepted local produce in exchange. The larger establishments provided the basis for a small mill village; at very favorable locations, a cluster of mills might create a small industrial town. At the top of the pyramid were the celebrated textile centers of New England, which at times had a score or more large-capacity mills, ranging in potential from a few thousand to 8,000 or 10,000 horsepower. The massive waterpower census survey of 1880, by which time auxiliary steampower was widely used to supplement waterpower, recorded at least a score of industrial communities of substantial size relying chiefly on waterpower. Perhaps as many as 40 or 50 developed waterpowers in the region east of the Mississippi and north of the Ohio River–Potomac River line were delivering as much or more power commercially to their customers as the celebrated Shaw's Water Works in Greenock, Scotland, described above.[31]

To analyze the causes, let us begin with the negative. About 75 years elapsed between the introduction of the Boulton & Watt rotative, or mill, engine before steampower took the lead in American manufacturing. This "backwardness" can hardly be attributed to ignorance or technical incompetence. The simple, compact, high-pressure, noncondensing engine developed by Oliver Evans, and taken over by other builders, had been on the market before 1810, both for stationary and steamboat use. While this engine rapidly became the predom-inant type in industry, the growth of stationary steampower

proceeded slowly. The first official survey of steampower in the
United States was made by the Department of the Treasury in
1838 because Congress was concerned with the rising level of
steam boiler explosions and casualties.[32] The 1,860 stationary
engines reported had an aggregate capacity of 36,000 horsepower and accounted for a little more than one-third (36 percent) of the total steampower in use.[33] Steamboat engines
constituted most of the remaining steampower, with 800 engines making up nearly three-fifths (57 percent) of the national
total of slightly more than 100,000 horsepower. On the basis of
the number of mills and manufactories reported in the 1840
census and the 1838 data, steampower accounted at this time
for no more than 10 to 15 percent of the aggregate stationary
power in manufacturing in the nation.[34]

The fairly detailed returns of the 1838 survey reveal some
surprising facts, concerning both the construction and use of
stationary engines, at this date predominantly mill engines. Of
nearly 1,100 engines for which information on place and name
of the builder is given, construction was distributed through 50
communities located in 16 states. If 100 single-engine builders
are excluded, the remaining 115 builders built an average of
eight engines each. Both construction and use of stationary
engines were greatly concentrated in a small number of large
cities. Four-fifths of the total number were built, and three-
fifths were in use, in the five large coastal cities from Boston to
Baltimore and the three large Ohio River cities: Pittsburgh,
Cincinnati, and Louisville.[35] Stationary steampower was an
urban phenomenon, for fairly obvious reasons: the opportunities presented by such predominantly commercial centers
for manufacturing and the almost total absence of waterpower
in these urban centers.

The reasons for the very limited use of stationary steampower in the late 1830s may be summarized very briefly: (1)
high initial costs; (2) unfamiliarity with operation, maintenance, and repairs; (3) high operating costs; (4) transportation
difficulties and costs for heavy equipment such as engines and
boilers; and (5) perhaps most important of all, the widespread,

familiar, and low-cost waterpower. The familiar litany of steampower's advantages over waterpower reflected the late-nineteenth-century conditions of rationalized production in a highly competitive market, with year-round, all-weather rail transportation serving all regions and most communities. They had but limited relevance for industry as conducted prior to the 1850s. Take mobility of steampower: as of 1830 at Pittsburgh, a 5-horsepower engine weighed nearly 1½ tons (2,800 lbs.); one of 60 horsepower, 16 tons.[36] Except along main-line water routes, the cost and difficulty of handling such heavy machinery was virtually prohibitive. Here, evidently, was a major reason both for the concentration of production and use of steam engines in a limited number of large urban centers, and for the low average output of engines per builder. Waterpowers, to exaggerate a bit, did not require mobility; in the lower ranges of capacity, as we shall see, they were everywhere! With the far slower tempo of enterprise in the prerailway age, growth capabilities were probably of a much lower priority of concern than in later years. The disadvantages of waterpower in terms of reliable supply were not very pronounced under the conditions of prerailway seasonality of trade, commerce, and industry alike, owing primarily to the seasonal character of inland transportation whether by road, river, or canal.[37]

In short, the adoption of steampower in industry was typically a solution of last resort, except where there was no alternative. That alternative was the waterpowers with which America was so amply supplied, and which, in the states of the North Atlantic Seaboard, were so well adapted to the needs of a pioneer economy moving slowly toward industrialization. The demographic and economic context contrasted with that of the mother country no less sharply than the geographic setting. In Britain, the advance of manufacturing followed centuries of agricultural evolution under the slowly working yeast of commercial enterprise and trade. The American people in the early decades of the nineteenth century were largely engaged not only in wresting a living directly from the land, but in extending the frontiers of settlement. The problem and the promise lay in the vast, unsettled lands to the west, in a population whose natural increase, supplemented by immigration, brought a doubling in numbers every 25 years, and in the immense task of converting a wooded wilderness to viable farms, and providing such basic community needs as roads, churches, schools, stores, and the like, which we have learned to call "infrastructure." American society, except in the older settled states of the northern seaboard, was overwhelmingly rural and agricultural, and thinly distributed over the eastern portions of a vast continent. As of 1840, the United States, with a land area of over 30 times that of England and Wales, had approximately the same population: 17 compared to 16 million. England and Wales were smaller in area than New England by one-eighth, but the British population distribution was far more dense (276 compared to 33 per square mile in America). Even the three southern and more developed New England states (Massachusetts, Connecticut, and Rhode Island) had a population density of only 88 per square mile. In the Middle Atlantic states of New York, New Jersey, and Pennsylvania, the population density was 44; and west of the Appalachians, in the five states north of the Ohio River and east of the Mississippi River, it fell to 12 per square mile.[38]

These figures highlight the wide differences in the conditions and problems faced by the two countries. In the United States, a pioneer but (in the later phrase) upwardly mobile people, because of their thin and widely scattered settlement and increasing remoteness from long-established coastal lines and centers of trade, were forced to rely on their own meager resources to survive and to advance their condition. The improvement of the primitive frontier transport facilities was far beyond local capabilities and could be only too slowly realized—perhaps over two or three generations—through outside initiative, enterprise, and private or public capital. The gradual extension of steam navigation on the larger river systems and inland waterways, east and west, from the early 1800s was followed in time by the extension of canal systems and turnpike roads. But even this progress was inadequate to serve the greater proportion of the population, which continued to lack direct access to such facilities. Not until the accelerating extension of railway facilities from the 1850s was a basis provided for a system of regional interchange and national markets, incorporating to a significant extent the great bulk of the more settled as well as the frontier communities. Before the Civil War, these communities were largely dependent upon their own resources, not only for the immense initial tasks of land clearance and farm building, but also for the early stages of emancipation from a subsistence economy.

The development of a simple grassroots "industrialism" to meet local needs for limited manufactured goods was a widespread American phenomenon of the early and middle decades of the nineteenth century. Escape from the limited range of simple products of the domestic and fireside industries was provided by local watermills for grinding grain and sawing lumber, the wares of itinerant craftsmen and peddlers, craft workshops, and varied specialized mills. Even a brief look through the published reports, or the unpublished schedules of the federal decennial censuses from 1820 through 1870, reveals convincing evidence of the widening range of small manufactories, listed county by county and state by state, and the astonishing national totals by quantity, if not by value, of the products. [39]

The rise of local manufactures in response to local need began in the community-based watermills, which before the end of the seventeenth century had come to be regarded as almost indispensable to the wellbeing of every pioneering settlement. Beginning typically with gristmills, followed shortly by sawmills, and in time, although less commonly, by carding and fulling mills, these rude but effective establishments were often erected with community encouragement and aid, and usually operated with no more than one or two hands. Such mills brought to frontier communities relief from some of the more laborious of the recurring tasks of every subsistence farm family. Hardly less important, they improved the quality of a product. The replacement of the coarse, uneven product of handmill or stump mortar by the meal or flour of the watermill, with their uniform and finer texture, was reflected in the taste of the foods made from them. So wide was the difference in comfort and convenience between the pioneer's hand-hewn log hut and the dwelling built from the sawmill's lumber which within a few years typically replaced it, that the first frame house in the community was remarked almost as often in local histories as the establishment of the first school, church or store.[40]

Watermills were but the first rung on the ladder in the upward climb from self-sufficiency. In a growing community, the increase of settlement and population was accompanied by the setting up of taverns, of stores with their initial meager stocks, of the workshops of shoemakers, clothiers, and blacksmiths, of carpenters, wheelwrights, and, with mounting maturity, a millwright to serve a wide radius of countryside.[41] According to circumstances of opportunity, need, and enterprise, in time quarries and brickyards might be opened, lime kilns of a sort, and even, though infrequently, potteries. More specialized types might follow, such as asheries, starch works, oil (linseed) mills, forges, furnaces and foundries, textile (yarn) mills of a hundred or so spindles, varied types of woodworking establishments (shingles, household wooden ware, containers). Such ventures were quite small in scale; they were prompted typically by local needs and favored by transport difficulties which excluded most outside competition. They depended on availability of local materials—timber, stone, clay, iron ore, the by-products of farming such as fats, hides, flax fibers, and sheep's wool, and the ashes produced by land clearing.[42] They provided outlets for small pockets of local capital and opportunities for ambitious and enterprising individuals and such malcontents as were produced by the hard labor and dull routine of farming.

From such slight beginnings, a slow upward spiraling of growth under favorable conditions of place and time was common. With the continued increase of settlement, the gradual improvement and rising productiveness of farming, the extension and improvement of local and outlying roads, supplemented occasionally by a turnpike and access to a canal system, markets widened, new enterprises appeared on the scene, and old ones grew in scale. All welcomed the rising diversification, including the farming community, eager to abandon the tedious household industries in exchange for coveted store goods which the widening outlet for farm produce—typically taken in trade to some extent by the local manufactories—made possible. In this way a multitude of small, largely autonomous economies multiplied over the land, and as transportation and marketing facilities improved prepared the way for connections with the regional economies which eventually emerged.

As manufacturing was recognized early as a necessary condition of growth and wellbeing, so waterpower was the prime, indeed indispensable, condition of the advance of manufacturing beyond the craft and workshop level. In contemporary discussion in such popular descriptive works as gazetteers, in the press, and as reflected in later histories of the pioneer experience, the attention devoted to millstreams and water privileges was second only to that given the agricultural resources, conditions, and activities predominant in most areas. Repeatedly, we come upon the familiar references to "an abundance of mill-seats," "the great facilities for mills," "the great advantages for hydraulic works," and the presence of "water machinery of various kinds." Although "mill rivers" were common enough, the millstreams most frequently mentioned were quite small affairs, often no more than creeks or brooks. Again and again we are told that a certain town "is abundantly supplied with mill-seats, although all its streams are small"; that a certain creek "and its numerous small streams afford an abundance of fine mill-seats and mills"; or that a town is "well-watered by springs, brooks and rivulets, the latter of a good size for mills." This was, of course, by no means a universal condition. Of a Vermont town settled in the 1780s, it was reported that for want of "water power, manufacturing establishments or central place of business, the occupation of the people has been exclusively confined to agriculture." In another instance there were "no streams of consequence and consequently no mills or mill privileges," a condition not without a silver lining "for the people are subjected to no expense for bridges nor loss by inundations." Unfortunate was the district with a "scarcity," a "scanty" or an "indifferent" supply of mill-seats, and where "the want of small streams . . . forbids the introduction of manufactures, except in the household way."[43]

In the literature of pioneering and economic development the waterpower upon which manufacturing depended is repeatedly identified with the determination of village and town sites. An early industrial historian declared that sawmills "followed the pioneer everywhere and formed with the grist mill the nucleus of every settlement neighborhood." Not only did colonial villages originate in mills, runs another account, but the location of most river towns was determined by waterpower. "The happy accident of water power in river or stream," declared an agricultural historian, "determined the location of most of the towns of inland New York as a thousand place names attest." An historian of the Old Northwest reported gristmills taking the lead in forming with sawmill, blacksmith shop, and store, "probably a village." To be near a suitable mill site, it was said of early Michigan, "was frequently a motive of settlement," while various mills and manufactories might be supplied "from the same cheap source of power." According to Merle Curti, "Almost all the villages of the [Trempeleau, Wisconsin] county were plotted at points deemed good for mill-sites."[44]

Manufacturing in the larger sense followed much the same pattern, as the history of innumerable mill villages in New England and elsewhere testifies. The manufacturing interests of this country, declared the widely traveled millowner of Rhode Island, Zachariah Allen, in 1829, "are all carried on in little hamlets, which often appear to spring up in the bosom of some forest, gathering around the water fall which serves to turn the mill wheel."[45] Out of the nearly 500 townships in the three states of southern New England—Massachusetts, Rhode Island, and Connecticut—according to Bidwell, "it would have been difficult [in 1840] to find 50 . . . which did not have at least one manufacturing village clustered around a cotton or woolen mill, an iron furnace, or a carriage shop."[46] Needless to say, steam engines were rarely the source of the necessary motive power. New England was preeminently the land of the mill or factory village, but the same pattern was found throughout the Middle Atlantic states and in diminishing degree through the industrially less advanced regions of the South and trans-Appalachian West. Moving upward in the scale of predominantly industrial communities as late as 1850, to that plateau occupied by the leading textile centers of inland New England, one looks in vain for those which are (except for coalmining towns and the Ohio River cities) largely dependent upon steampower.

How admirably the supply of waterpower was adapted to the needs it served becomes evident from a closer look at stream flow, the source of energy to which millwheels by the tens of thousands were once harnessed. One must probe beyond the conventional notion that the key element in waterpower was the waterwheel itself, even when, as occasionally noted, supplemented by the milldam and millpond and the supporting structure of the mill. This was the characteristic viewpoint of the millwright, who knew better but took the rest for granted and, quite understandably, that of the historian, who does not. The base point of waterpower, as pioneer America well knew, was the break in the stream-bed constituting the mill-seat or water privilege of this discussion; but the engineer recognized that the true foundation of waterpower lay in the closely identified association of the hydrologic cycle and the drainage basin.[47] The former was the endlessly recurring cycle of rainfall, evaporation, plant transpiration and, above all, the residuary "runoff" which with the area of the stream's drainage basin so largely determined the volume of stream flow and its waterpower potential.

The whole land, save for the dead-ends of swamp and marsh-land, was an intricate yet orderly system of streams with their drainage basins, the larger of which had their outlets in the sea. Many of the affluents, especially in New England, had their sources in ponds or lakes, natural reservoirs serving as useful regulators of stream flow, storing up water during periods of rain and snowfall for gradual later release. The pattern of the river system, large or small, was that of the widespreading tree with its trunk, its limbs, its branches and branches of branches, proliferating in number and decreasing in size as one advanced from the mainstream to the outer reaches of the smallest branches within the drainage basin of the whole.

The brooks and creeks constituting the smallest class of millstreams were not only the most numerous by far, but the most widely distributed and the most readily brought under power development. They were tributaries alike of the "trunk," the "limbs," and the larger and lesser "branches" of the river system. Volume of flow increased with advance from the outlying to the central and lower portions of the system. In matters of such importance for a stream's power potential as average slope of stream bed (in feet per mile), or frequency of occurrence of waterfalls or rapids (mill-seats), occasioned by irregularities in geological formations and the available amount of fall at each, there was little uniformity. Yet in any sizable river system, the number of waterpowers was more or less in inverse ratio to their capacity. By and large, as one moved from the main river to its principal tributaries and to the affluents of these in turn, once, twice, or thrice removed, the number of waterpowers increased and their average capacity decreased in something like geometric progression. In the northeastern United States, whose hilly and mountainous terrain was so admirably adapted to waterpower, there was only one Niagara, a few score powers in the range of 1,000 to 10,000 or more horsepower capacity, on down to many thousands of powers capable of meeting the modest needs of the common water-mill.[48]

As examples of waterpower at the high plateau of its development in the United States, although already in relative decline in the face of the rapidly growing shift to steampower, two of the leading waterpower basins in the country in 1880 will serve to illustrate the wide range of utility of this ancient source of power.[49] The Merrimack River, in its day variously described as "the most noted water power river" and "the hardest worked river" in the world, in 1880 supplied about 900 mills and factories with an aggregate of nearly 80,000 horsepower. The fame of this stream rested primarily on the three leading textile centers situated at intervals along the lower half of the Merrimack's 110-mile course through New Hampshire and Masschusetts. The 29,000 horsepower divided fairly evenly among Lowell, Lawrence, and Manchester, marked the use of waterpower on a magnitude unapproached elsewhere before the coming of hydroelectricity and far above the average at the vast majority of industrial establishments in New England. Counting only the leading textile corporations in the three Merrimack River centers, 21 companies, employing on an average more than 1,000 horsepower each, together accounted for 25,000 of the 29,000 water/horsepower in use at the three cities. The 15 leading tributaries of the Merrimack together had nearly 27,000 horsepower in use, divided among some 380 mills, or an average of 70 horsepower. The direct tributaries, secondary tributaries, and their affluents in turn, together supplied more than 500 mills with a total of some 23,000 horsepower and an average rating of 45 horsepower. The several hundred mills on the lesser streams lumped under "other tributaries" had an average rating of 31 horsepower, reflecting the small scale of these industrial establishments.

The progression from larger to lesser powers which marks the difference in capacities, as we move from the trunkline to the lesser tributaries, is repeated with variations in the other great waterpower basins of the Northeast. In the Hudson River system, the largest single developed power was at Cohoes,

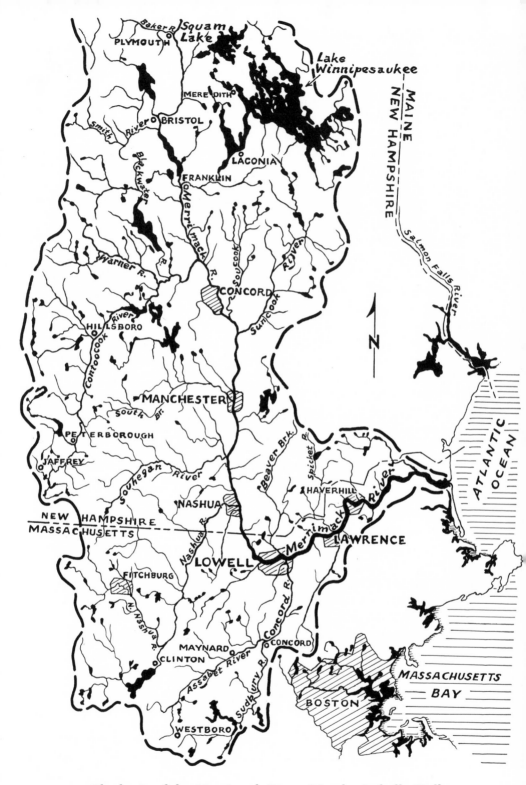

The basin of the Merrimack River. Map by Isabella Walker.

near the mouth of the Mohawk, with 6,500 horsepower. Although slightly greater in aggregate developed waterpower than the Merrimack River, the Hudson River had a drainage basin three times as large. The range in power capacity per mill, from the trunkline of the Hudson to the lesser tributaries, was from about 250 to 25 horsepower; 24 of the 38 streams in the Hudson River system had one-half the aggregate developed power, but accounted for three-fourths of the total number of mills. The average per mill was but 32 horsepower. At the other extreme, the half-dozen largest streams in developed waterpower had but one-eighth the total number of mills but nearly three-fifths the aggregate horsepower, so that the average per mill was 141 horsepower or more than four times as large.

In short, the arrangements of nature were in substantial accord with the requirements of a slowly emerging industrial economy, beginning with the numerous and widely distributed small establishments. In response to such trends as the growing density of population, improvements in the facilities of transportation, widening range of markets, extension of mechanization, and improvements in production methods, the trend moved toward progressively larger establishments and power requirements. This led to a searching out and development of powers capable of meeting the larger demands, and culminating in the commercial development and sale of power at such great waterpowers as those on the Merrimack River—Lowell, Lawrence, Manchester—and the Connecticut River at Holyoke and Bellows Falls. Within the range of available choice in any area, waterpowers varied widely in respect to such important considerations as accessibility, engineering and construction difficulties, expense, regularity and reliability of stream flow, and flood hazards. Yet even in 1880, when many of the larger industrial centers in New England had exhausted their waterpower and were employing more or less auxiliary steampower, there were still within the region numerous large undeveloped waterpowers. The 1880 census survey listed 16, ranging from 2,000 to 13,000 gross horse-power capacity.[50]

Two further points will conclude this brief review of the long continued reliance of American industry, at all levels, upon waterpower. They consider the persistence of the traditional technology in the use of waterpower, and the increasing resort from the 1850s on to steampower in an auxiliary capacity. Next to the ubiquitous character of waterpower and the long-standing familiarity with its use, the compelling factor in its early and long continued use was the widespread availability of the materials and skills needed for its development and freedom from the capital outlays typically required by steam engines and associated iron millwork, even had such machinery been within reach by available transport facilities. From its very beginnings, water-power had rested upon the centuries-old craft technology of wood and the associated arts and crafts of masonry and earthwork. The dams and supporting facilities and structures, raceways, penstocks, millwheels, and wheel installations were all a heritage from the distant past. The millwheels, and in the prefactory mills the accompanying gearwheels and shafting, were made largely if not wholly of wood. In the mill building and such related structures as dams, abutments, and retaining walls, the timber and the fieldstones and boulders used in the rough masonry were drawn from the immediate neighborhood and assembled with the traditional craft skills and tools. Because of scarcity, cost, and difficulty of working, iron and other metals were typically limited to bearings, reenforcement bands, and fastenings. To the ancient crafts of carpenter and joiner were added, when available, such other crafts as that of the shipwright, wheelwright, blacksmith, and especially that predecessor of the mechanical engineer, the millwright. All these artisans were skilled in their several ways in the arts of cutting, shaping, fitting, and joining wood; the blacksmith worked with iron. In the larger and more carefully built mill-works, rough-hewn or simply felled timber, trimmed of limbs and branches, gave way to dimension timber, hewn or sawn, while rough-set stonework was replaced by dressed masonry.

In the prime movers themselves, in the largest mills of the Lowell type, as in the numberless country mills, wooden waterwheels of the traditional types continued the rule, reaching impressive dimensions and weights in the huge breastwheels of the largest textile mills. While iron components such as wheel shafts or gudgeons, hub-spiders, and bolts slowly made their way into the larger installations, the breast and overshot wheels long continued to be made chiefly of wood.[51] The shift to iron came with the introduction of the turbine wheel, which because of the complexity of its design and its many parts, was necessarily made entirely of iron. First introduced in the late 1840s, and within a decade or so produced widely in foundry and factory, turbines demonstrated their superiority to the old-style wheels on virtually all counts: compactness, durability, high running speeds, efficiency, and low cost. They gradually replaced the older wheels at all but the smallest mills. An 1886 survey showed that in 47 New England cottonmills the ratio of breast and overshot wheels to turbines was 88 to 119; the Massachusetts state census of 1875 reported nearly four-fifths of all waterwheels used in manufacturing were turbines.[52] The replacement of the wooden millwork of the country mill by iron gearwheels and shafting had taken place decades earlier in all but the smallest mills.

Steampower in manufacturing made its way slowly in the older industrial regions of the Northeast and in districts and establishments hitherto on waterpower, chiefly in an auxiliary capacity. (Tables 1 and 2, pages 191–92) Even before 1850, steampower was being introduced to supplement waterwheels, at first usually to meet power shortages in the low water seasons, but sooner or later in expanding establishments to obtain additional year-round capacity. With the widening experience and familiarity with steampower and the increasing availability of steam engines, the principal obstacle to its use was higher cost—both initial outlay in the smaller capacities and high operating costs in large installations. James B. Francis as chief engineer and superintendent of the Locks and Canals of Lowell, proprietors of the waterpower system, and as consultant to the textile corporations, owner-users of this power, followed the trend of steampower improvements and costs closely. His careful calculations in the mid-1850s based for steampower on data supplied by George Corliss of Providence, builder of the engine bearing his name, showed steampower as costing three times as much as waterpower, as the cost of the latter was reckoned at the Merrimack River textile centers.[53]

Ten years later, improvements in steam-engine efficiency had narrowed the ratio to 2 to 1; by 1880 the Lowell mills used more steam than water horsepower, despite advances in the overall capacity of the Lowell waterpower system.[54] By this time, resort to auxiliary steampower had become widespread in most districts relying chiefly on waterpower. In the river basins tributary to Long Island Sound, including the Connecticut, and in the Hudson River basin, steampower, as reported by the census of 1880, provided one-fifth of the aggregate power in use in manufacturing.[55] It was not uncommon in many mills for a reversal of roles, with the original waterpower capacity assigned the auxiliary share.

On the continent of Europe, the experience of France, falling within the mainstream of Western European development, provides a useful comparison to the British and American examples, especially insofar as geographic considerations are concerned. France was the first large continental country to undergo industrialization, standing in important respects well apart from the nations of Central and Southern Europe. Four times as large as England and Wales combined, France had not only extensive coastlines on the Atlantic and Mediterranean, but also, two of her land frontiers were mountainous areas, marked by the Pyrenees and the Alps.[56] Owing to close proximity and long historical associations, France drew largely on British industrial experience, especially with respect to technology, technicians, and capital. More favored than Britain in timber and wood resources, France's coalfields were far smaller and poorly located with reference to other industrial requirements. This circumstance, together with the disposition of other physical features and resources and the large size of the country, created major transportation problems which affected the scale of firms, until resolved by the creation of a railway network.[57]

In waterpower, on the other hand, with her extensive mountain frontiers and such internal highlands favorable to stream flow as the Jura, Vosges, and Massif Central, combined with extensive river systems, France led the countries of Western Europe. The greater part of this potential energy, remote from areas of need, awaited the day of hydroelectricity for its realization. It was upon the thousands of small waterpowers along the hundreds of lesser streams whose drainage basins blanketed the land that manufacturing enterprise in the early stages of industrialization largely depended. French industry turned early to steampower in some districts and industries. Arrangements were made with Watt himself for building engines on his plan in France; but the scarcity and cost of coal led manufacturers in France as well as elsewhere on the continent to prefer Woolf's compound engine for its fuel economy. Initially discouraged in England by the inability to use Watt's condenser, the builders of the Woolf engine found a welcome market in France.[58] By 1850, the 6,800 steam engines reported for France outnumbered, by one estimate, steam engines in all the other continental countries combined.[59] Yet steampower was hardly relevant to the power needs of the great majority of small firms constituting the expanding industrial base of France. In the 1860s when in the United States steampower was overtaking and passing waterpower, in France it accounted for less than one-third of the total industrial motive power.

The choice of power reflected a variety of circumstances and conditions prevailing in any district: scale of operations, power requirements, availability and cost of fuel, frequency and scale of waterpowers, and level of industrial organization and technology. Falling water as the traditional power source attracted the attention of scientists and engineers as well as private and public agencies concerned with promoting industrial growth. Much attention was directed to improving the efficiency of waterwheels to offset the limited scale of most waterpowers, and awards were established to this end. Poncelet received one for his distinctive and effective undershot wheel with curved floats. The experiments of Burdin and Fourneyron culminated in the perfecting and practical introduction of the turbine, also the recipient of an award, from the 1830s on the most important nineteenth-century innovation in waterwheels.

In his study of the Industrial Revolution in France to 1848, Dunham found that in most industrial districts except the Nord, and in marked contrast to the British practice, waterpower was the usual reliance. The cost of fuel and the slow progress toward large integrated firms on the English pattern were the chief causes, but transportation difficulties and the traditional practices of the district and industry were influential. Dunham felt it necessary to add, having in mind the tendency to identify steam power with industrial advance, that reliance upon waterpower "was not detrimental to industrial progress provided the supply of water was adequate and the wheel or turbine was efficient."[60]

The comprehensive industrial census of 1861–65 gives a clear panoramic view of French industry, arranged in 16 *grandes divisions* or groups. In four leading industries—textiles, extractive (mining), metallurgical, and metal working—taken together, steampower led waterpower in the ratio of 2 to 1 for horsepower capacity (the average per establishment was 20 and 12 horsepower, respectively). Yet in the overall balance, these "large" industries were outweighed by the grain-milling industry alone. Here water mills outnumbered steam mills 20 to 1 and in aggregate horsepower 9 to 1. Overall, waterpower exceeded steampower in the ratio of 2 to 1; if windmills and horse-powered mills are added to water mills, the ratio rises to 2¼ to 1. From the 1860s to the end of the century the course of motive power in French industry was much the same as in the United States, except that the shift from water to steampower in France was even more rapid than here.[61]

With the notable exception of Belgium, the advance of industrialization elsewhere on the Continent proceeded very slowly, all the countries relying largely on waterpower as in France, until late in the century. The English economist, Thomas C. Banfield, has left a graphic picture of steampower's gradual but disturbing penetration of the Rhineland, for want of waterpowers of adequate capacity to serve as the necessary agent of centralized production on the English plan.[62] Perhaps the most impressive evidence of waterpower's persistent vitality is the leading role of Western Europe in developing the striking new modes of power transmission as means of bringing into use hitherto inaccessible waterpowers. Both the teledynamic system developed by C. F. Hirn of Alsace in the 1850s, of transmitting power by fast-moving wire ropes for distances up to several miles and the pioneer electric transmission installations from the 1880s were for years employed chiefly in the development of waterpower in the fuel-scarce regions of Switzerland and adjoining areas in France and Germany.[63]

In the perspective of American and Continental experience, seen against the background of British industrialization, the traditional view of stationary steampower as the central and well-nigh indispensable agent of the Industrial Revolution loses much of its persuasiveness. It is probable that when all the returns are in from all the major participants in the nineteenth-century drive toward industrialization, the pattern of British experience will prove to be the exception rather than the rule. Understandably, the appearance of a new source of motive power, seemingly under man's complete control as to time, place, and amount, was received with wonder and an almost worshipful enthusiasm. The intricacy of the steam engine's mechanical arrangements, the automaticity of its behavior, its identification with the extraordinary achievements in mining, textiles, and metals, and in time its adaptation to the requirements of transportation on land and sea, combined to elevate steampower in this first industrial nation to the status of a mystique. In sober retrospect the mystique of motive power, whether supplied by wind, water, or steam, dissolves. Instead, factors of technique and geography, and the basic economic considerations of availability and cost, stand out in high relief.

Table 1.

Abstract from returns respecting steamboats, locomotives, and stationary engines.

	Number of steamboats	Number of locomotives	Number of stationary engines
Maine	8	2	41
New Hampshire	1	–	6
Vermont	4		
Massachusetts	12	37	165
Rhode Island	2	–	58
Connecticut	19	6	47
New York	140	28	87
New Jersey	21	32	32
Pennsylvania	134	96	383
Delaware	3	14	11
Maryland	19	31	56
District of Columbia	5	–	13
Virginia	16	34	124
North Carolina	11	5	20
South Carolina	22	27	40
Georgia	29	3	23
Florida	17	2	8
Alabama	18	1	40
Louisiana	30	10	274
Arkansas			
Mississippi			
Tennessee			
Kentucky, (including part of Indiana,)	41	2	
Missouri and Illinois	42	–	56
Indiana, (included, in part, in Kentucky.)			
Ohio	79	1	83
Michigan and Wisconsin (in part)	13	6	32
Iowa			
United States Government	14	–	17
Total ascertained	700	337	1,616
Add, as estimated	100	13	244
Aggregate	800	350	1,860

Whole number of steam-engines of all kinds ascertained is 2,653, and estimated 357; making the aggregate 3,010.

The above estimate is added for the States of Tennessee, Arkansas, Illinois, Indiana, and some omissions in other States, with the Territory of Iowa, and part of Wisconsin. In New York, it is believed that one or two more locomotives are running, but I have not yet been able to obtain accurate returns of them.

SOURCE: Treasury Department inquiry of 1838, "Document No. 21," pp. 376 and 379, showing the number, type and regional distribution of the major categories of steam engines: steam vessels, railroad locomotives and stationary ("standing") engines, the aggregate capacity in horsepower standing in sharp contrast with some 50,000 water-mills of all types returned by the Census of 1840.

Table 2.
STANDING STEAM-ENGINES IN EACH STATE

States	Number	Power	Period first introduced into use in the State
Maine	41	765	1833
New Hampshire	6	102	1833
Massachusetts	165	2,244	1827
Connecticut	47	315	1830
Rhode Island	58	1,430	1828
Vermont		None returned.	
New York	87	1,425	
New Jersey	32	516	1787 to 1834
Pennsylvania	383	7,448	1791 to 1810
Delaware	11	88	1825
Maryland	56	683	1818
District of Columbia	13	206	1827
Virginia	124	1,567	1821
North Carolina	20	751	1821
South Carolina	40	675	1819
Georgia	23	799	1827
Florida	8	215	1833
Alabama*	40	800	
Louisiana	274	7,796	1821
Missouri and Illinois, in part	56	1,120	1837 and 1838
Ohio	83	1,786	1818
Michigan	32	368	1828
Tennessee			
Indiana, and			
Kentucky		None returned.	
Wisconsin			
Iowa			
United States Government	17	340	
	1,616	31,439	
Add standing engines not returned, but estimated	244	4,880	
Total	1,860	36,319	

*These are, in some degree, estimated by the collector.

SOURCE: See Table 1, page 191.

NOTES

Charles F. Carroll (pages 13–36)

1. The forest cover of the northeastern United States before the European discovery is described in Margaret B. Davis, "Phytogeography and Palynology of Northeastern United States," in H. E. Wright, Jr., and David G. Frey, eds., *The Quaternary of the United States* (Princeton, N. J., 1965), pp. 386–97. A description of early America from an ecological point of view is presented by Victor E. Shelford, *The Ecology of North America* (Urbana, Ill., 1963). Among the numerous works dealing with the American Indians are Harold E. Driver, *Indians of North America*, 2nd ed. (Chicago, 1969); and Clark Wissler, *The Indians of the United States: Four Centuries of their History and Culture* (New York, 1940).

2. Edmund S. Morgan, *The Puritan Dilemma: The Story of John Winthrop* (Boston, 1958), pp. 18–53; Joshua Scottow, *A Narrative of the Planting of the Massachusetts Colony Anno 1628* (Boston, 1694), p. 9.

3. Carl Bridenbaugh, *Vexed and Troubled Englishmen, 1590–1642* (New York, 1968), pp. 394–433; Nellis M. Crouse, "Causes of the Great Migration, 1630–1640," *New England Quarterly* 5 (1932): 3–36; George C. Homans, "The Puritans and the Clothing Industry in England," *New England Quarterly* 13 (1940): 519–29; Charles F. Carroll, *The Timber Economy of Puritan New England* (Providence, R. I., 1973), pp. 7–10.

4. Carroll, *Timber Economy*, pp. 10–13. The actual size of some of the woodlands in Essex can be estimated from John Norden's map in *Speculi Britanniae Pars: An Historical and Chorographical Description of the County of Essex*, 1594, ed. Sir Henry Ellis, Camden Society, Publication no. 9 (London, 1840).

5. *Winthrop Papers, 1498–1649*, 5 vols. (Massachusetts Historical Society, Boston, 1929–47), 1: 296–98; Sumner Chilton Powell, *Puritan Village: The Formation of a New England Town* (Middletown, Conn., 1963), pp. 41, 55–57.

6. John White, *The Planters Plea, Or The Grounds of Plantations Examined, And Usuall Objections answered* (London, 1630), pp. 21–22; "Papers of Sir John Eliot," *Proceedings of the Massachusetts Historical Society*, 8 (1864–65): 418–26; Joshua Scottow, *A Narrative of the Planting of the Massachusetts Colony Anno 1628* (Boston, 1694), p. 12; [Francis] Higgeson [Higginson], *New-Englands Plantation, or a Short and True Description of the Commodities and Discommodities of that Countrey*, 3d ed. (London, 1630), no pagination.

7. James Kendall Hosmer, ed., *Winthrop's Journal*, 2 vols. (New York, 1908), 1:47; "Good News from New-England," (London, 1648), in *Massachusetts Historical Society Collections*, 4th ser., 1(1852):200.

8. For interpretations of Puritan attitudes toward expansion into the wilderness, see Alan Heimert, "Puritanism, the Wilderness, and the Fron-

tier," *New England Quarterly* 25 (1953): 361–82, and Peter N. Carroll, *Puritanism and the Wilderness: The Intellectual Significance of the New England Frontier, 1629–1700* (New York, 1969), esp. pp. 140–47.

9. "Good News from New-England," p. 201; J. Franklin Jameson, ed., *Johnson's Wonder-Working Providence, 1628–1651* (New York, 1910), p. 112; William Wood, *New Englands Prospect* (London, 1634), pp. 44–45; Daniel Neal, *The History of New England,* 2 vols. (London, 1720), 2:574; Capt. John Smith, *Advertisements for the unexperienced Planters of New-England or any where* (London, 1631), pp. 29–30.

10. Wood, *New Englands Prospect,* pp. 46–47; John Josselyn, *An Account of Two Voyages to New England* (London, 1674), pp. 29, 117, 121–22; "Good News from New-England," p. 202.

11. Smith, *Advertisements,* pp. 28–29; Pond to William Pond, Mar. 15, 1631, *Proceedings of the Massachusetts Historical Society,* 2nd ser., 8(1892–94):471; *Winthrop Papers,* 1:165–66.

12. Hosmer, ed., *Winthrop's Journal,* 1:54, 58; Jameson, ed., *Johnson's Wonder-Working Providence,* pp. 65, 114; Wood, *New Englands Prospect,* p. 47; "Capt. Roger Clap's Memoirs," in Alexander Young, ed., *Chronicles of the First Planters of the Colony of Massachusetts Bay, from 1623 to 1636* (Boston, 1846), pp. 348–49, 351; "Autobiography of Michael Wigglesworth," *New England Historical and Genealogical Register,* 17 (1863):137; E. B. O'Callaghan, ed., *Documentary History of the State of New York,* 4 vols. (Albany, N.Y., 1849–51), 4:31; Hugh Morrison, *Early American Architecture: From the First Colonial Settlements to the National Period* (New York, 1952), p. 9.

13. Jameson, ed., *Johnson's Wonder-Working Providence,* p. 114.

14. Smith, *Advertisements,* p. 27; Joseph Schafer, *The Social History of American Agriculture* (New York, 1936), pp. 38–39; Jameson, ed., *Johnson's Wonder-Working Providence,* p. 196.

15. William Douglass, *A Summary, Historical and Political of the . . . British Settlements in North America,* 2 vols. (Boston, 1749–51), 2:53.

16. Samuel Symonds to John Winthrop, Jr., Dec. 14, 1637, *Winthrop Papers,* 3:518; Jameson, ed., *Johnson's Wonder-Working Providence,* p. 196. Gabriel Thomas, *An Historical and Geographical Account of the Province and Country of Pensilvania; and of West-New-Jersey in America* (London, 1698), p. 8, claims that "two men may clear between Twenty and Thirty Acres of Land in one Year, fit for the Plough." It is very doubtful, however, that a busy farmer could completely clear ten acres in a year.

17. Robert Trow-Smith, *A History of British Livestock Husbandry to 1700* (London, 1957), pp. 16–18, 41–42, 198, 233, 250–51; Pond to William Pond, Mar. 15, 1631, p. 471; *A Treatise of New England Published in Anno Dom. 1637 and Now Reprinted* (n.p., 1650; photostat in the John Carter Brown Library, Brown University, Providence, R.I.), pp. 2–3; "Trelawny Papers," in *Documentary History of the State of Maine,* 24 vols. (Portland, Me., 1869–1916), 3(1884):30–32, 46, 57, 109, 141; *Winthrop Papers,* 3:121.

18. Hosmer, ed., *Winthrop's Journal,* 1:105; "Trelawny Papers," p. 141.

19. Powell, *Puritan Village*, p. 12; Wood, *New Englands Prospect*, p. 41.
20. *Dorchester Town Records, Fourth Report of the Record Commissioners* (Boston, 1880), pp. 1–2; *The Records of the Town of Cambridge (Formerly Newtowne) Massachusetts, 1630–1703* (Cambridge, Mass., 1901), pp. 8, 30–31; Nathaniel B. Shurtleff, ed., *Records of the Governor and Company of Massachusetts Bay in New England,* 5 vols. (Boston, 1853–54), 1:181–82, 188–89, 219–20, 238–39, 255, 317.
21. Harold R. Shurtleff, *The Log Cabin Myth* (Cambridge, Mass., 1939); Morrison, *Early American Architecture*, pp. 12–13.
22. Hosmer, ed., *Winthrop's Journal*, 1:55, 77, 90; Morrison, *Early American Architecture*, pp. 14–15, 35; John Demos, *A Little Commonwealth: Family Life in Plymouth Colony* (New York, 1970), pp. 24–35; *The Early Records of the Town of Dedham,* 6 vols. (Dedham, Mass., 1886–1936), 3:25; Francis Kirby to John Winthrop, Jr., 1632, *Winthrop Papers*, 3:99; Meyric R. Rogers, *American Interior Design* (New York, 1947), pp. 51–52; "A Note-Book Kept by Thomas Lechford, Esq., Lawyer, in Boston, Massachusetts Bay, from June 27, 1638 to July 29, 1641," in *Transactions and Collections of the American Antiquarian Society,* 7(1885): 94–100, 363–64. Also see John Fitchen, *The New World Dutch Barn: A Study of Its Characteristics, Its Structural System, and Its Probable Erectional Procedures* (Syracuse, N.Y., 1968).
23. Jameson, ed., *Johnson's Wonder-Working Providence*, p. 39; *Winthrop Papers*, 4:108, 145; Wood, *New Englands Prospect*, p. 43; *Records of the Town of Dedham*, 1:37; Hosmer, ed., *Winthrop's Journal*, 1:83, 115, 137.
24. The problems of early iron manufacture at Lynn and Braintree are covered in Edward Neal Hartley, *Ironworks on the Saugus* (Norman, Okla., 1957). However, Hartley does not emphasize that it was the high cost of procuring wood and turning it into charcoal that led to the failure of the ironworks. See Saugus Ironworks, Account Books, Baker Library, Harvard Business School, Allston, Mass., esp. pp. 43–113.
25. The fur trade, as well as the desire for agricultural land, lured settlers into the interior. Lancaster and Springfield were founded as fur-trading posts, and the fur trade was an influence in the settlement of Concord, Chelmsford, Groton, Marlborough, Sudbury, and Northampton. See Francis X. Moloney, *The Fur Trade in New England, 1620–1676* (Cambridge, Mass., 1931), pp. 46–78.
   No less than 300,000 cod were caught in the Massachusetts Bay region in 1641 (Hosmer, ed., *Winthrop's Journal*, 2:42, 306–07). It is probable, however, that much of this catch was brought in by the Marblehead and Hull fishermen who had been making similar catches all through the 1630s. According to Ralph Brown, *Historical Geography of the United States* (New York, 1948), p. 25, a dozen men could catch 20,000 to 25,000 fish a month. Therefore, only 150 men would be needed to catch 300,000 fish a month. Also see Bernard Bailyn, *The New England Merchants in the Seventeenth Century* (Cambridge, Mass., 1955), pp. 23–26, 49–60, 76–78.
26. Francisco Morales Padron, *El Comercio Canario-Americano (Siglos*

XVI, XVII y XVIII) (Sevilla, 1955), pp. 22–25, 297; Hans Sloane, *A Voyage to the Islands Madera, Barbados, Nieves, S. Christophers and Jamaica*, 2 vols. (London, 1707–25), 1:9–10; Frédéric Mauro, *Le Portugal et l'Atlantique au XVII Siècle* (1570–1670) (Paris, 1960), pp. 183–89, 299, 352–56; F. Andrew Michaux, *The North American Sylva; or A Description of the Forest Trees of the United States, Canada, Nova Scotia. Considered Particularly with Respect to Their Introduction into Commerce*, 3 vols. (Philadelphia, 1859), 1:26, 85.

27. The best description of cooperage is: Auguste-Denis Fougeroux de Bondaroy, *Art du Tonnelier* (Paris, 1763), in Académie des sciences, Paris, *Descriptions des Arts et Métiers, faites ou approuvées par messieurs de l'Académie royale des sciences*, 45 vols. (Paris, 1761–88).

28. Darrett B. Rutman, *Winthrop's Boston: Portrait of a Puritan Town, 1630–1649* (Chapel Hill, N.C., 1965), pp. 184–85; *A Volume . . . Containing the Aspinwall Notarial Records from 1644–1651* (Thirty-Second Report of the Record Commissioners of the City of Boston) (Boston, 1903), pp. 71–72; Hosmer, ed., *Winthrop's Journal*, 2:68, 72, 126–27.

29. *Winthrop Papers*, 1:345, 356–57, 361–62, 382, 405; Carl and Roberta Bridenbaugh, *No Peace Beyond the Line: The English in the Caribbean, 1624–1690* (New York, 1972), ch. 3; Richard Ligon, *A True & Exact History of the Island of Barbados* (London, 1657), pp. 85–86; Sir Dalby Thomas, *An Historical Account of the Rise and Growth of the West-India Collonies* (London, 1690), pp. 15–20; Richard S. Dunn, "The Barbados Census of 1680: Profile of the Richest Colony in English America," *William and Mary Quarterly* 3rd ser., (1969): 11, 16; Richard S. Dunn, *Sugar and Slaves: The Rise of the Planter Class in the West Indies, 1624–1713* (Chapel Hill, N.C., 1972), pp. 287–94.

30. Abbot Payson Usher, *A History of Mechanical Inventions*, rev. ed. (Cambridge, Mass., 1954), pp. 184–86; John W. Dean, ed., *Capt. John Mason, The Founder of New Hampshire* (Boston, 1887), pp. 284, 289, 306, 310–12.

31. For a discussion of the various sawmills built in New England during this period, see Charles F. Carroll, "The Forest Society of New England: Timber, Trade, and Society in the Age of Wood, 1600–1688," (Ph.D. dissertation, Brown University, 1970), pp. 383–549.

32. Robert Greenhalgh Albion, *Forests and Sea Power: The Timber Problem of the Royal Navy 1652–1862* (Cambridge, Mass., 1926), pp. 29, 31, 96, 164–68, 218, 234.

33. *Aspinwall Notarial Records*, pp. 13–14, 143, 185; *Calendar of State Papers, Domestic Series, 1649–1650*, p. 317; 1651, p. 507; 1653–1654, pp. 163, 253, 317; William B. Weeden, *Economic and Social History of New England 1620–1789*, 2 vols. (Boston, 1890), 1:56; Albion, *Forests and Sea Power*, pp. 51–52, 56, 218; Nathaniel Bouton, et al., eds., *Documents and Records Relating to the Province of New Hampshire*, 40 vols. (Concord, N.H., 1867–1943), 17:515.

34. Carroll, *Timber Economy*, pp. 90–95.

35. *Ibid.*, p. 131.

36. *Ibid.*, pp. 131–34. The shifting patterns in the trade of New England in the seventeenth century are covered in detail there on pp. 87–97.

37. The early legal battles over the control of timber and timberland are in Bouton, *et al.*, *Documents and Records Relating to the Province of New Hampshire*, vol. 40.

38. Carroll, *Timber Economy*, pp. 102–09.

39. *Clarendon Papers, Collections of the New-York Historical Society* (1869), pp. 71–72, 79–80, 138–39; Shurtleff, ed., *Records of the Governor and Company of Massachusetts Bay*, vol. 4, pt. 2, pp. 318, 327–28, 368–70, 538.

40. Randolph's career is covered in Michael Garibaldi Hall, *Edward Randolph and the American Colonies*, 1676–1703 (Chapel Hill, N.C., 1960); and in R.N. Toppan and T.S. Goodrick, *Edward Randolph: Including His Letters and Official Papers*, 1676–1703, 7 vols. (Boston, 1898–1909). For the problems of New Hampshire under the new government, see Jeremy Belknap, *The History of New-Hampshire*, 3 vols. (Dover, N.H., 1812), 1:150–51, 318; H.L. Osgood, *The American Colonies in the Seventeenth Century*, 3 vols. (New York, 1904–07), 3:338–56.

Nathan Rosenberg (pages 37–62)

1. Tench Coxe claimed in 1810 that the potash and pearlash derived in clearing the trees of new farmland for cultivation would "nearly compensate the settler" for the expenses thus incurred, at least where the land was "convenient for boat navigation." Tench Coxe, *A Statement of the Arts and Manufactures of the United States of America* (1810), p. xvii. For a similar earlier statement, see Tench Coxe, *A View of the United States of America* (Philadelphia, 1794), p. 454.

2. Lewis Mumford, *Technics and Civilization* (New York, 1934), pp. 119–20.

3. See *Eighth Census of United States: Manufactures*, pp. 733–42. Value added by manufacture was $54,671,082 for cotton goods and $53,569,942 for lumber.

4. Nathan Rosenberg, "Innovative Responses to Materials Shortages," *American Economic Review Papers and Proceedings* (May 1973).

5. John Richards, *A Treatise on the Construction and Operation of Woodworking Machines* (London, 1872), p. iv.

6. *Ibid.*

7. *Ibid.*, p. 33.

8. Victor Clark, *History of Manufactures in the United States*, 3 vols., (New York, 1929), I, 48.

9. James Elliot Defebaugh, *History of the Lumber Industry of America*, 2 vols., (Chicago, 1907), II, 9.

10. Roger Burlingame, *March of the Iron Men* (New York, 1938), p. 39.

11. J. Leander Bishop, *A History of American Manufactures from 1608 to 1860*, 3 vols., (Philadelphia, 1868), I, 492. See also Albert S. Bolles, *Industrial History of the United States* (Norwich, Conn., 1878), pp.

218–21. The number cited by Bishop is suspiciously high. Bolles refers to a machine perfected in 1810 "which was able to make a hundred nails a minute."

12. Bolles, p. 220. Temin points out that, in colonial days, abandoned houses were often burned down in order to recover the nails. Peter Temin, *Iron and Steel in Nineteenth Century America* (Cambridge, 1964), p. 42.

13. Fogel has pointed out, in criticizing Rostow's overemphasis upon the railroad demand for iron, that " . . . in 1849 the domestic production of nails probably exceeded that of rails by over 100 per cent." Robert Fogel, *Railroads and American Economic Growth* (Baltimore, 1964), p. 135.

14. For a later period (1872) one very well informed observer estimated that three-quarters of all woodworking machinery in America was devoted to the preparation of building materials. Richards, p. 48.

15. Siegfried Giedion, *Space, Time and Architecture* (Cambridge, 1941), p. 347.

16. *Ibid.*, pp. 347–55.

17. The Census of 1810 reported 2,541 sawmills. In addition to its other deficiencies, however, this census provided only partial coverage including, e.g., no report on sawmills in Connecticut, New Hampshire, New York, North Carolina, and Vermont. All that can be said, therefore, is that the total number of sawmills must have greatly exceeded the number cited.

18. Defebaugh, I, 490.

19. Fred H. Gilman, "History of the Development of Saw Mill and Woodworking Machinery," *Mississippi Valley Lumberman* (February 1, 1895), p. 61.

20. Rodney C. Loehr, "Saving the Kerf: The Introduction of the Band Saw Mill," *Agricultural History* (July 1949), pp. 168–69.

21. *Ibid.*, p. 169.

22. *Niles Weekly Register*, July 19, 1817, p. 336, reported that the sawmill of Stewart and Hill of Baltimore had installed a rapid circular saw for cutting veneers. It pointed out, significantly, that "two boys may attend the machine."

23. Defebaugh, II, 442.

24. Richards, p. 141.

25. G. L. Molesworth, "On the Conversion of Wood by Machinery," *Proceedings of the Institution of Civil Engineers*, vol. 17, 1857–58, p. 22. Richards stated that English saws in 1860 were, on the average, half the thickness of American saws. John Richards, "Woodworking Machinery," *Journal of the Franklin Institute* (June 1870), p. 399. See also M. Powis Bale, *Woodworking Machinery*, 2nd ed. (London, 1896), pp. 327–28.

26. For many years large, usable wood scraps had been simply burned. "The slab butts and edgings of boards were carried outside of the mills and board piles, and thrown into a common pile to be burned and which was kept constantly burning, winter and summer. Thus millions of slabs were burned to get rid of them, and the burning did not entirely cease until

about 1835 or 1840, although the best of them were cut into lath or were used for other purposes much earlier." Defebaugh, II, 443.

27. *Niles Weekly Register*, March 27, 1819, p. 93, and also Sept. 28, 1833.

28. Loehr, p. 169.

29. Richards, pp. 207–39.

30. *Special Report of Mr. Joseph Whitworth* (1854) as reprinted in Nathan Rosenberg, *The American System of Manufactures* (Edinburgh, 1969), p. 345.

31. Bale, pp. 88–89.

32. "Mortises and tenons represent in wood work what bolts and rivets do in metal work, —the mechanical means of connecting the different parts of frames and structures: the analogy is, however, far from complete. Metals are joined by fusion or welding; they are also connected without special reference to fibre, while in wood work all connections or joints must be mechanical, and every piece arranged with strict reference to its fibre. Transversely, it has no capacity for withstanding tensile strain, at least none that need to be practically considered, while parallel with the fibre its coefficient compares with many metals. Its employment, however, to resist tensile strain is rendered impracticable, or nearly so, from the want of some means of connecting its ends, so as to represent a continued strength throughout such joints." Richards, p. 239.

33. *Ibid.*, p. 243. The reciprocating mortising machine was an excellent example of American boldness in machinery design. Richards states: "To develop the reciprocating mortising machine, as it has been done in America, requires three things: highly-skilled labour, a long experience, and very limited amount of engineering knowledge with the builders of the machines. This last condition is rather a curious one, but a skilled engineer, conversant with all the principles of the operation and difficulties to be encountered in making and using such machines, could not conscientiously recommend them, except for the lighter class of work . . . "

34. *Report of the Committee on the Machinery of the United States*, in Rosenberg, *The American System of Manufactures*, p. 171.

35. *Whitworth Report* in *ibid.*, p. 344. The *Report of the Committee on the Machinery of the United States* had observed: "The several parts of a house are got up in separate manufactories, such as stairs and staircases. Here there is every appliance for bending and twisting the wood, and working it under awkward forms. For doors, window-frames, and sashes. For this purpose special tools are employed for mortising, tenoning, and forming the moulding," *loc. cit.*

36. See *ibid.*, pp. 29–36.

37. Dwight Goddard, *Eminent Engineers* (New York, 1905), p. 73. See also the detailed description provided by the British parliamentary committee, which observed them in operation in Springfield in 1854, in Rosenberg, *The American System of Manufactures*, pp. 137–43. Whitworth, in his report, provided a precise breakdown of the total labor time consumed at Springfield Armory in making gunstocks by machinery. He

reported that all the operations together took just over 22 minutes of labor time. *Ibid.*, p. 365.

38. Asa Waters, *Biographical Sketch of Thomas Blanchard and his Inventions* (Worcester, 1878), p. 8. It was later claimed that the Blanchard lathe was originally invented in England. See, for example, D. K. Clark, *The Exhibited Machinery of 1862*, London Exhibition, 1864, p. 221. No evidence whatever is provided in support of the assertion. But, in any case, it is clear that if some neglected English mechanical genius had invented a similar machine, he had absolutely no influence on subsequent developments. When British engineers first examined American woodworking machinery in the early 1850s, they acclaimed the Blanchard lathe as a wonderful invention, unknown to them, and purchased large numbers of them from the Ames Manufacturing Company in Chicopee, Massachusetts, for use in the Enfield Arsenal. And their Report had stated: "It is most remarkable that this valuable labor-saving machine should have been so much neglected in England, seeing that it is capable of being applied to so many branches of manufacture, its introdution into the armoury will prove a national benefit." Reprinted in Rosenberg, p. 138.

39. Charles Fitch, "Report on the Manufactures of Interchangeable Mechanism," *Tenth Census of the United States*, 1880, II, 14.

40. An amusing account of European incredulity is provided by Zachariah Allen: "On my way from Brussels to Haerlem to view the national exhibition of the manufactures of Belgium, holden under the auspices of the king and honoured by his presiding at the distribution of the prizes, having accidentally fallen into company in a diligence with a Flemish artist on his way to the same place with some of his new machines, our conversation turned upon the subject of steam navigation, then lately introduced into that country. He inquired if there were any steamboats in America, and was surprized on being informed that they had been in successful operation there nearly twenty years. I took occasion to describe to him several American inventions, among others the machine for cutting and heading nails, which are completely finished and fall from the engine as fast as one can count them. The machine for making weavers reeds or slaies seemed to strike his attention as a wonderful invention, whereby the mechanism is made to draw in the flattened wire from a reel, to insert it between the side pieces, to cut it off at the proper length, and finally to bind each dent firmly in its place with tarred twine, accomplishing the whole operation without the assistance of the attendant, in a more perfect manner than can be performed by the most skillful hand. Although he possessed a good share of intelligence, the complicated operations of these machines, performing processes which he supposed could only be brought about by manual dexterity, appeared to him incomprehensible. But when I proceeded to describe Blanchard's lathe in which gun stocks and shoe lasts are turned exactly to a pattern, his belief seemed somewhat wavering, and on continuing to give him a description of Whitmore's celebrated Card Machine, which draws off the card wire from the reel, cuts it off at a proper length for the teeth, bends it

into the form of a staple, punctures the holes in the leather, and inserts the staples of wire into the punctures, and finally crooks the teeth to the desired form—performing all these operations with regularity without the assistance of the human hand to guide or direct it, the credulity of my travelling companion in the diligence would extend no farther, and he evidently began to doubt all the statements I had been making to him, manifesting at the same time some little feeling of irritation at what he appeared to consider an attempt to impose upon him such marvellous accounts. Uttering an emphatic humph! he threw himself back into the corner of the diligence, and declined further conversation during the remainder of our ride upon the subject of mechanics and of the improvements made in Flemish manufactures." Zachariah Allen, *The Science of Mechanics* (Providence, R. I., 1829), pp. 348–49. The incident occurred during Allen's continental tour in 1825.

41. "In those districts of the United States of America that the Committee have visited the working of wood by machinery in almost every branch of industry, is all but universal; and in large establishments the ordinary tools of the carpenter are seldom seen, except in finishing off, after the several parts of the article have been put together.

"The determination to use labour-saving machinery has divided the class of work usually carried on by carpenters and the other wood trades into special manufactures, where only one kind of article is produced, but in numbers or quantity almost in many cases incredible." *Report of the Committee on the Machinery of the United States*, as reprinted in Rosenberg, p. 167.

42. The extent to which Blanchard's lathe wasted wood may well have been the critical factor in the British failure to show more interest in it until the later, improved models were developed. Thus, an experienced London gunmaker, who was questioned concerning stockmaking machinery by the Parliamentary Select Committee on Small Arms, replied: "The first stock machine that I ever saw was introduced into England 20 years ago, an American invention; it was sent over here, a beautiful working model of it, and submitted for purchase right of working it to all the gun-makers here, and it was forwarded from London to Birmingham, and there a very eminent manufacturer, and a very extensive one, brought it into active operation, but he found that the guns that cost him 1 s. for stocking by machinery he could do for 7 d. and 8 d. by hand labour, the waste in that machinery is so very great. This working model we had in Pall Mall, it was in the shop of the elder Mr. Wilkinson at the time; there were pieces of wood of about 18 inches long that were fixed in, and you saw the stock turned and worked." "Yet the loss of material was so great that it was discontinued?" "Yes." *Report from the Select Committee on Small Arms*, Parliamentary Papers, 1854, vol. XVIII, Q. 7273 and Q. 7274. See also Q. 7520 and Q. 7521, and Molesworth, pp. 22, 45–46.

43. See A. William Hoglund, "Forest Conservation and Stove Inventors 1789–1850," *Forest History*, (Winter 1962). Hoglund states that, in spite of much criticism of stoves, fireplaces had come to be regarded as "old-fashioned" by the 1840s.

44. Louis Hunter, *Steamboats on the Western Rivers* (Cambridge, 1949), pp. 130–33.
45. "Lumber manufacture, from the log to the finished state, is, in America, characterized by a waste that can truly be called criminal . . . " Richards, p. 141.
46. This trade-off was, to some degree, also influenced by the crudeness of design and manufacture of machinery during this period.

Charles E. Peterson (pages 63–84)

1. Nathan Rosenberg, *Technology and American Economic Growth* (New York, 1972), pp. 27–31.
2. A recent collection of source material on sawmilling and the lumber trade may be found in Charles E. Peterson, "Sawdust Trail," *Association for Preservation Technology Bulletin*, vol. 5, no. 2 (1973), 84–151.
3. Herbert C. Wise and H. Ferdinand Beidleman, *Colonial Architecture for Those about to Build* (Philadelphia and London, 1913), p. 15.
4. Samuel Smiles, *Industrial Biography, Iron Workers and Tool Makers*, (London, 1863), pp. 165–166.
5. Peterson, p. 94.
6. *Ibid.*, p. 102.
7. William P. Fox, *A History of the Lumber Industry in the State of New York*, (Washington, 1902), pp. 12, 13.
8. *Colonies, Series C-13-A*, 4-P 1018, (Paris, Archives Nationales) (Ms. courtesy of Samuel Wilson, Jr.).
9. Christopher Roberts, *The Middlesex Canal*, 1793–1860 (Cambridge, 1938).
10. "Rules and Regulations of the Government of the Middlesex Canal," 1808, broadside, Massachusetts Historical Society, Boston.
11. Typescript at Henry Ford Museum, Dearborn.
12. Thomas Anburey, *Travels through the Interior Parts of North America in a Series of Letters*, (London, 1789), I, 313, 317, 349.
13. John Pell, "Philip Skene of Skenesborough," *Quarterly Journal of the New York State Historical Association*, IX (1928), 27–44.
14. Oliver Evans, *The Young Mill-Wrights' & Millers' Guide* (Philadelphia, 1795).
15. Greville Bathe, *An Engineer's Note Book* (St. Augustine, 1955), p. 22.
16. Rita Susswein Gottesmann, *The Arts and Crafts in New York*, 1800–1804 (New York, 1965), pp. 200–01.
17. *Ibid.*, p. 428.
18. Greville Bathe and Dorothy Bathe, *Oliver Evans* (Philadelphia, 1935), pp. 73, 132.
19. *Association for Preservation Technology, Bulletin* vol. II, nos. 1–2 (1970) contains a large collection of source material on early shingles and other types of roofing.

Silvio A. Bedini (pages 85–119)

1. For a history of the use of navigational instruments, see David W. Waters, *The Art of Navigation in England in Elizabethan and Early Stuart Times* (London, 1958); for a descriptive handbook of their function, see H.O. Hill and E.W. Paget-Tomlinson, *Instruments of Navigation* (London, 1958).

2. In the collection of the Peabody Museum, Salem, Mass.

3. *Boston Gazette*, Aug. 22–29, 1737; Nov. 21–28, 1737; Dec. 25, 1774.

4. *Boston Gazette*, May 19–26, 1740.

5. In the collection of the New London County Historical Society, New London, Conn.

6. F. Lewis Hinckley, *Directory of the Historic Cabinet Woods* (New York, 1960). See under the various woods described.

7. Silvio A. Bedini, *Early American Scientific Instruments and Their Makers* (Washington, 1964), pp. 65–79.

8. *Ibid*, pp. 117–19.

9. *Ibid*. pp. 34–36. See also LeRoy E. Kimball. "James Wilson of Vermont. America's First Globe Maker," *Proceedings of the American Antiquarian Society* (April 1938), New Series vol. 48, no. 1, pp. 29–48.

10. Bedini, pp. 15–17, 39–41. Harrold E. Gillingham, "The First Orreries In America," *Journal of the Franklin Institute*, vol. 229, 1940, 229, 92–97.

11. A copy is in the collection of the John Carter Brown Library, Brown University, Providence, R.I.

12. *Boston Gazette*, Feb. 16, 1789.

13. Anthony N.P. Garvan, "Review of Early American Scientific Instruments and Their Makers," *Technology and Culture*, 1965, vol. 6, pp. 464–465.

14. For a detailed study of the appreticeship system in colonial America, see Robert Francis Seybolt, *Apprenticeship & Apprenticeship Education in Colonial New England and New York* (Teachers College Columbia University Contributions to Education, No. 85, New York, 1917).

15. Bedini, pp. 75–79.

16. Philip F. Purrington, "Taking Lunars on Water Street," *The Bulletin of the Old Dartmouth Historical Society and Whaling Museum* (Spring 1959), pp. 2–4.

17. This essay is based in large part on the writer's forthcoming new work on the mathematical practitioner movement in America entitled *Thinkers and Tinkers: Early American Men of Science* (New York, 1975).

Louis C. Hunter (pages 160–192)

1. Elijah Galloway, C.E., *History of the Steam Engine From Its Earliest Invention to the Recent Time*. 2nd. ed. (London, 1828), p. 61.

2. Thomas Ewbank, quoted in *American Artisan*, July 18, 1866.
3. On the early history of watermills in the western world, the following are particularly useful: L. A. Moritz, *Grain Mills and Flour in Classical Antiquity* (Oxford, England, 1958); Lynn White, Jr., *Medieval Technology and Social Change* (Oxford, England, 1962); Richard Bennett and John Elton, *History of Corn Milling*, 4 vols. (London and Liverpool, 1898–1904); chapters on *Power* by R. J. Forbes in Charles Singer, *et al.*, *A History of Technology*, 5 vols. (Oxford, England, 1954–58). The following articles are of particular value: E. C. Curwen, "The Problems of Early Water-Mills," *Antiquity*, 18–19 (1944–45), 130–46; B. Gille, "Le Moulin à eau: une révolution technique médiévale", *Techniques et civilisation*, 3 (1954); and Marc Bloch, "The Advent and Triumph of the Water-Mill," in *Land and Work in Medieval Europe. Selected Papers by Marc Bloch* (New York, 1969). For the persistence of the traditional watermills down to the present time in the underdeveloped portions of Southern and Eastern Europe, see L. C. Hunter, "The Living Past in the Appalachias of Europe," *Technology and Culture*, 8 (1967), 446–66, with photographs.
4. T. K. Derry and T. L. Williams, *A Short History of Technology* (New York, 1961).
5. Melvin Kranzberg and Carroll W. Purcell, Jr. *Technology in Western Civilization*, Vol. 1 (New York, 1967). This neglect is in part remedied by Eugene S. Ferguson in the chapter, "The Steam Engine Before 1830," which suggests the possible geographic limitations upon water-power in Britain. The Marx and Engels quotation is taken from Ivan Melada, *The Captain of Industry in English Fiction, 1821–1871* (Albuquerque, 1970), p. 1
6. For this development in the United States, see George R. Taylor, *The Transportation Revolution, 1815–1860* (New York, 1951); for Great Britain, see H. J. Dyos and D. H. Aldcroft, *British Transport. An Economic Survey from the Seventeenth Century to the Twentieth* (Leicester, England, 1969).
7. Since the substantial impact of steampower in transportation upon industry and the economy generally was not felt before 1850, discussion of the earlier years may properly be concentrated on the field of stationary power with which this essay is concerned. Tonnage of steam vessels in the United States rose from some 24,000 in 1825 (U.S. population, 11.2 million) to 200,000 in 1840 and 480,000 in 1850 (U.S. population, 23.3 million). For the British Empire, corresponding tonnage figures for the three dates were 20,000, 87,000, and 167,000. L. C. Hunter, *Steamboats on the Western Rivers* (Cambridge, Mass., 1949), table 1, p. 33. Railway mileage in the United States rose from 2,800 in 1840 to 9,000 in 1850 and 31,000 in 1860. *Historical Statistics of the United States, 1789–1945* (Washington, 1945), p. 200. Similar data for Great Britain are given in Dyos and Aldcroft, *British Transport, op. cit.*, pp. 124ff.
8. The problem of regularity of motion, on which the satisfactory performance of most industrial operations to some degree depends, results typically from appreciable changes in load imposed by the machinery on

the prime mover. So far as the prime mover itself is concerned, the waterwheel with its continuous rotary motion is more favorable to regularity of motion than the steam engine, whose reciprocating action results in a continuously changing force upon the piston. These variations are not wholly overcome by the flywheel employed with most steam engines. The development of effective and sensitive governors to provide the uniformity of motion so important in most industrial operations has been a critical problem in the development of modern prime movers.

9. On the use of rods, races, and pipes for the transmission of power in mining regions, see J.S. Courtanay, "A Treatise on the Statistics of Cornwall," *Sixth Annual Report of the Royal Cornwall Polytechnic Society*, 1838, pp. 93, 108–09; Anthony Rouse, "Overshot Water Wheels Employed in Pumping Water at Wheal Friendship Lead and Copper Mines near Tavistock," *Prcdgs. Instit. Civil Engrs.*, 2, Session 1842, 97ff.; T.J. Bewick, C.E., F.G.S., "On Mining in the Mountain Limestone of the North of England," *Trans. N. of Engl. Inst. Mining and Mechan. Engrs.*, 18 (1868–69), 164–82. For interesting examples of the use of waterpower in mining, including long, contour-course supply channels, see D. Morgan Rees, *Mines, Mills and Furnaces. An Introduction to Industrial Archeology in Wales* (London, 1969).

10. According to Peter Mathias, no point in England is more than 70 miles from the sea and, in the early eighteenth century, "very few were more than 30 miles from navigable water." Peter Mathias, *The First Industrial Nation* (New York, 1969), p 109.

11. R.W. Finn, *Introduction to Domesday Book* (New York, 1963), pp. 187ff; and Margaret T. Hodgen, "Domesday Water Mills," *Antiquity*, vol. 13 (1939).

12. Robert Leslie, London, September 26, 1793, to Oliver Evans, cited in Greville and Dorothy Bathe, *Oliver Evans* (Philadelphia, 1935), pp. 41–42; see also pp. 50–51. A similar report was made by Zachariah Allen in 1825: *The Practical Tourist* (Providence, 1832), I, 32–33.

13. Rex Wailes, leading authority on the history of windmills in Britain, to author: London, Oct. 9, 1958.

14. The distances given here have been taken from the American edition of *Chambers's Encyclopaedia* (Edinburgh, 1880), titled *Library of Universal Knowledge*, 15 vols. (New York, 1881), by name of river.

15. I.D. Stamp and S.H. Beaver, *The British Isles. A Geographic and Economic Survey*, 2nd ed. (London, 1937).

16. Frederick Brown, "Significant Trends in the Development and Utilization of Power Resources: Great Britain," *Trans. Third World Power Conference*, 11, (Washington, 1938), 587. This figure, totaling 218,000 KW, covered establishments employing more than ten persons.

17. Zachariah Allen, the Rhode Island manufacturer, visiting Britain in 1825 remarked: "It seems that water power, wherever found, is highly valued in England; but from the inadequate supply of water falls in this country to operate the enlarged mills required at the present day to manufacture with all the advantages accruing from extensive machinery and due subdivisions of labor, &c., the additional power of steam engines has

been resorted to." From *The Practical Tourist* (Providence, 1832), I, 347.

18. Article, "Water Power," *Library of Universal Knowledge*, 15 (New York, 1881), 286–88; and William Fairbairn, *Treatise on Mills and Millwork*, Pt. 1 (London, 1861), 126ff.

19. There are many accounts of the Greenock installation. One of the earliest is that of Loammi Baldwin in his *Report on the Subject of Introducing Pure Water into the City of Boston* (Boston, 1834), pp. 18ff. Following a visit to Shaw's Water Works in July 1849, James B. Francis of Lowell's Locks and Canals described the installation in a letter of Nov. 24, 1849, printed in *Hunt's Merchants Mag.*, 22 (1850), 32: see also article on "New System of Water Power," reprinted from *New Monthly Magazine for* 1829 in *Jour. Frkln. Inst.*, 11 (1831), 212–15. By this account, the method employed at Greenock originated at Rothsay on the Isle of Bute; the capacity of the Greenock installation, here given as 2,000 hp, could be increased to 3,000 hp and the system could be readily adapted to other sites. Further details are given in Joseph Glynn, *Rudimentary Treatise on the Power of Water* (London, 1853), pp. 28–30. At the lower end of the falls, where both lines of fall were combined to serve the needs of a large cotton mill, there was installed what in overall dimensions, if not in capacity, was probably "the largest, or nearly the largest waterwheel in existence," 70 ft. 2 in. diameter and 13 ft. wide, as compared with the celebrated Burden wheel of the same suspension type of construction of Troy, New York, with its 62 ft. diameter and 20 ft. width. See *Library of Universal Knowledge*, 15, 288–89, "Water Power." For the Burden wheel, see F.R.I. Sweeny, "The Burden Water-Wheel," Society for Industrial Archeology, *Occasional Publications*, No. 2 (April 1973), from *Trans. ASCE*, 1915.

20. The inquisitive reader must make his way through the underbrush of frequently conflicting tabular data in a variety of works among which the following may be noted, in order of their appearance: Edward Baines, *History of the Cotton Manufacture in Great Britain* (London, no date: preface, 1835), Ch. XI, and pp. 388ff; Andrew Ure, *Philosophy of Manufactures* (London, 1835), opp. p. 480; James Wheeler, *Manchester* (London, 1836), pp. 208–09; H.D. Fong, *The Triumph of the Factory System in England* (Tientsin, China, 1930) pp. 35, 63, 86, 101; J.H. Clapham, *An Economic History of Modern Britain* (London, 1932), vol. 1, pp. 441–43; and last and in many respects the best: M. Balug, "The Productivity of Capital in the Lancashire Cotton Industry During the Nineteenth Century," *Econ. Hist. Review* (April 1, 1961), pp. 358ff.

21. Jennifer Tann, *The Development of the Factory* (London, 1970) pp. 59–61.

22. A.H. Dodd, *The Industrial Revolution in North Wales* (Cardiff, 1933), p. vii, 142, 153, 246–51, 265–72; and A.H. John, *The Industrial Development of South Wales, 1750–1850* (Cardiff, 1950), especially chapters 4–6.

23. J.D. Marshall, *Furness and the Industrial Revolution* (Barrow-in-Furness, 1958) pp. 17, 38, 51–54, 195ff., 203–06, 223ff.

24. R.H. Hills, *Power in the Industrial Revolution* (New York, 1970), Ch. 6, "Natural Sources of Power."
25. F. Braithewaite, "On the Rise and Fall of the River Wandle," *Prcdgs. Instit. Civil Engrs.*, 20, Session 1860–61, 191ff., including the discussion following the paper which materially amplifies it. See a related paper by James Charles Clutterbuck, "The Perennial and Flood Waters of the Upper Thames," *ibid.*, 22, Session 1862–63, 336–70. The portion of the Thames above Oxford covered here extends some 30 miles with an average fall per mile of 19½ inches. Including the mills on 8 tributaries "and others," the total number of manufactories was 144.
26. Phyllis Deane, *The First Industrial Revolution* (Cambridge, England, 1965), pp. 132–33.
27. The standard authority here is T.S. William, *River Navigation in England, 1600–1750* (Reprint edition, New York, 1965). For a more comprehensive treatment of inland transportation, see Dyos and Aldcroft, *British Transport*. On the relation of transportation facilities to industrial development in England, see Mathias, *The First Industrial Nation*, pp. 106ff.
28. Fred S. Thacker, *The Thames Highway*, Vol. 1 (Reprint Edition, New York, 1968), 3. The extent of the joint use of other English rivers by milling and navigation interests is not clear, but the practice evidently was by no means confined to the Thames. See Willan, *River Navigation in England*, pp. 47–52. Specific references to the "corn" or flour mills suggests that they ranged typically between two and five "run" or pairs of millstones which at some 5 horsepower per run gives an aggregate power requirement of no more than 20–25 horsepower. The "falls" occurring in the riverbeds seem typically to have been no more than pronounced rapids with the necessary aggregate fall at the mill obtained by long contour-course headraces, often evidently of a mile or more. See "Water Power," *Library of Universal Knowledge* (American ed. of *Chambers's Encyclopaedia*, 1880; New York, 1881), 15, 286–89; and A. Newell, *A Hillside View of Industrial History. A Study of Industrial Evolution in the Pennine Highlands* (Todmorden, no date), pp. 235–54.
29. Thacker, *op. cit.*, I, 5.
30. The data on numbers of establishments which follow have been drawn from the Federal decennial census records, published or manuscript schedule, 1840–1880; the numerous state gazetteers from the 1830s; and the comprehensive two-volume survey conducted in connection with the Tenth Census, 1880, under the Census Office: *Reports on the Water-Power of the United States* (Washington, 1885 and 1887).
31. A list of the largest developed waterpowers in the United States, with various particulars, is given in *ibid.*, pt. 1, xxx–xxxii.
32. "Report on the Steam Engines in the United States," Document No. 21, 25th Cong. Third Sess. (Serial 345).
33. Making allowance for certain omissions in the coverage of the survey (which was based on enumeration for the greater part of the country, estimates for areas not readily reached) would bring the total number to

perhaps 2,000, with an addition of nearly 4,000 horsepower to the overall total.

34. These estimates, based on estimated average power requirements of different types of mills and manufactories, are the author's.

35. The author's compilation and analysis of the data in the 1838 report.

36. Letterbook #2, Kingsland, Lightner and Company, (Pittsburgh: Western Pennsylvania Historical Society), p. 191, June 11, 1832. Frequent reference is found in the correspondence of this foundry firm to the difficulties of shipment of heavy machinery which steamboats at times were quite reluctant to accept. (The 16-ton weight here noted probably included boilers as well as engines.) The 18-ft. diameter flywheel alone weighed 5,000 lbs. *Ibid.*, pp. 87, 93, March 20, 1829.

37. The seasonal conditions of trade and industry are dealt with in some detail in L.C. Hunter, *Studies in the Economic History of the Ohio Valley* (Northampton, Mass., 1934).

38. Population and area data are taken from *Historical Statistics of the United States to* 1957 (Washington, 1960), and 13; and *Encyclopaedia Britannica*, 9 (11th ed., New York, 1911), 404.

39. The following figures from contemporary gazetteers and histories, 1820–24, give the aggregate numbers of grist, saw, fulling, and carding mills and tanneries with the state populations in rounded thousands following in parentheses: Maine: 1,877 (298): Vermont 1,902 (236); New Hampshire: 2,504 (244); and New York: 9,689 (1,373). According to the 1840 census, there were in the United States, with its population of just over 17 millions, 23,611 gristmills and 31,650 sawmills; fulling mills and tanneries numbered 2,585 and 8,229 respectively. *Compendium of the Enumeration of the Inhabitants and Statistics of the United States* (Washington, 1841), pp. 36–64.

40. "Among the pleasures, furnished by the melioration of their circumstances," declared President Timothy Dwight of Yale College of the pioneers, "the exchange of their log-hut for decent houses must not be forgotten." Timothy Dwight, *Travels in New England and New York,* 2 (New Haven, 1821–22), 469.

41. According to a leading Vermonter describing in 1848 the advances in this remote and rugged state from the self-sufficiency of each homestead, the only trades then deemed indispensable were those of the shoemaker and blacksmith, themselves also farmers. With time the early hardships were mitigated and life became easier: "As the condition of the people improved, they by degrees, extended their desires beyond the necessaries of life; first to its conveniences and then to its elegancies. This produced new wants; and to supply these, mechanics more numerous and more skillful were required, till at length the cabinet maker, the tailor, the jeweler, the milliner and a host of others came to be regarded as indispensable." Zadock Thompson, *Geography and Geology of Vermont* (Burlington, 1848), pp. 112–13.

42. See Tench Coxe, "A Statement of the Arts and Manufactures of the United States of America," June 21, 1813, Philadelphia, *American State Papers, Finance,* 2, 666ff.

43. Among the more useful of the state gazetteers for the older states are Zadock Thompson for Vermont, 1824; John Farmer and Jacob B. Moore for New Hampshire, 1823; Horace C. Spafford for New York, 1813, 1824; John Hayward for Massachusetts, 1846, 1849; Thomas F. Gordon for Pennsylvania, 1832, New Jersey, 1834, and New York, 1836; Warren Jenkins for Ohio, 1837; and John T. Blois, for Michigan, 1838.

44. The authorities cited here include A.S. Bolles, V.S. Clark, U.P. Hedrick, L.D. Stilwell, S.W. Fletcher, and R.C. Buley.

45. *The Science of Mechanics* (Providence, 1829), p. 352.

46. Percy W. Bidwell, "The Rural Economy of New England at the Beginning of the Nineteenth Century," *Trans. Connecticut Academy of Arts and Sciences,* 20 (1916), 241ff.

47. For an account of the hydrologic cycle and other aspects of stream flow bearing upon waterpower, see the brief, carefully done articles in *Water. The Yearbook of Agriculture,* 1955. United States Department of Agriculture (Washington, no date), 41ff., 52ff. The engineering conception of waterpower resources is the frame of reference in which the 1880 census survey of water power was carried out (and which contrasts with that of the millwright as reflected, for example, in the classic handbook of Oliver Evans, *The Young Millwright and Miller's Guide* [Philadelphia, 1795, and numerous later editions]); it was published as *Reports on the Water-Power of the United States, Census Office, Department of the Interior,* 2 vols. (Washington, 1885, 1887). (Courtesy of Meyer Fishbein, The National Archives.)

48. See, for example, the lists of large developed and undeveloped powers in the United States listed in *ibid.*, Pt. 1, pp. xxx-xxxv.

49. The data which follow on the waterpower of the several river basins noted have been compiled from appropriate portions of the 1880 census survey on waterpower here cited and reported in great detail, river by river.

50. *Ibid.*, Pt. 1, pp. xxxiii-xxxv.

51. For the design and fabrication of the traditional types of waterwheels, see any edition of Evans, *Young Millwright and Miller's Guide*. British manufacturers and millwrights were well in advance of American practice in respect to the use of iron in the waterwheels and millwork of the larger class of mills with John Smeaton in the late eighteenth and William Fairbairn in the early nineteenth century leading the way. See articles in the *Dictionary of National Biography*.

52. New England Cotton Manufacturers' Association, *Statistics of Cotton Manufacturers in New England,* 1866 (Boston, 1866), No. 1; C.D. Wright, *The Census of Massachusetts,* 1875, 2 (Boston, 1877), 325.

53. James B. Francis to Corliss and Nightingale, Providence, R.I., Jan. 6, 1854; additional memoranda, Jan. 13, 1854, and July 22, 1854; Papers, Locks and Canals, Vol. A-2, Manuscript Division, Baker Library, Harvard Business School. The 1876 estimate is found in Francis to T.O. Selfridge, Sept. 1, 1876, *ibid.*, DB-9, 16–17.

54. Francis to James Powell, May 3, 1881, *ibid.*, DB-11, 103-04. "Nearly all of the water-mills in operation today," declared a speaker at an 1880

gathering of the New England Textile Manufacturers, "have outstripped the capacity . . . of the streams where they are located." *Water Power of the U.S.*, *op. cit.*, Pt. 1.

55. In the tabular statements summarizing the waterpowers for many of the river basins surveyed, a column is provided for "auxiliary steam power," with total figures in some instances provided. On the significance of the term as used here see *ibid.*, pp. 328–29.

56. Henri Sens, *Les Forces hydrauliques des Pyrénées* (Paris, 1926), pp. 26–28.

57. The following works are particularly useful for their discussion of French industrial development: R.F. Cameron, *France and the Economic Development of Europe*, 1800–1914 (Princeton, N.J., 1961); A.L. Dunham, *The Industrial Revolution in France*, 1815–1848 (New York, 1955); and W.O. Henderson, *Britain and Industrial Europe* (Liverpool, 1954). For an illuminating contemporary account of the penetration of Germany by the English methods of organization and production, marked by the substitution of steam for waterpower, see Thomas C. Banfield, *Industry on the Rhine* [1846, 1848] (reprint edition, New York, 1969).

58. Henderson, *Britain and Industrial Europe*, pp. 43ff., 58ff.

59. Cameron, *France and the Economic Development of Europe*, pp. 66–67.

60. Dunham, *The Industrial Revolution in France*, Ch. 5, "Fuel and Power," pp. 85–118.

61. From the early 1860s to 1901, steam power increased elevenfold, while waterpower less than doubled. Steampower's share of the combined total of these two leading power sources rose from 31 percent to 77 percent during this period. *Statistique de la France: Industries, Résultats généraux de l'enquête effecturée dans les années 1861–1865* (Nancy, 1873), pp. xiiiff. These totals do not include the cities of Paris and Lyons nor the Établissements de l'État. For 1901 and later years, see Michel Huber, "La Statistique des forces motrices," *Jour. de Statistique de la Société de Paris* (November, 1932), p. 403.

62. Thomas C. Banfield, *Industry on the Rhine* [Agriculture, 1846; Manufactures, 1847] (New York, reprint edition, 1969). I am indebted to Selma Thomas for this reference.

63. Useful sources on these matters are William C. Unwin, *On the Development and Transmission of Power from Central Stations* (London, 1894), and Gisbert Kapp, *Electric Transmission of Energy*, 3rd ed. (London, 1891), especially chapters IX and XII.

FURTHER READINGS

As the contributors to this volume have pointed out, the literature on America's Wooden Age is scant, though growing. Two works which provide annotated bibliographies of the growth of early American technology are Brooke Hindle, *Technology in Early America* (Chapel Hill, N.C., 1966) and Eugene S. Ferguson, *Bibliography of the History of Technology* (Cambridge, Mass., 1968).

The following list offers some suggestions for further reading on the main topics covered in this volume.

Settlement and Development of Northern New England

Jeremy Belknap. *The History of New Hampshire*, 3 vols. Dover, N.H., 181w.

Charles E. Clark. *The Eastern Frontier: The Settlement of Northern New England, 1610–1763.* New York, 1970.

William G. Saltonstall. *Ports of the Piscataqua.* Cambridge, Mass., 1941.

Jasper Jacob Stahl. *History of Old Broad Bay and Waldoboro*, 2 vols. Portland, Me., 1956.

Development of the Lumbering Industry

Robert Greenhalgh Albion. *Forests and Sea Power: The Timber Problem of the Royal Navy, 1652–1862.* Cambridge, Mass., 1926.

Bernard Bailyn. *The New England Merchants in the Seventeenth Century.* Cambridge, Mass., 1955.

Charles F. Carroll. *The Timber Economy of Puritan New England.* Providence, R.I., 1973.

James Elliot Defebaugh. *History of the Lumber Industry of America*, 2 vols. Chicago, 1907.

F. Andrew Michaux. *The North American Sylva; or A Description of the Forest Trees of the United States, Canada, Nova Scotia. Considered Particularly with Respect to Their Introduction into Commerce*, 3 vols. Philadelphia, 1859.

Victor E. Shelford. *The Ecology of North America.* Urbana, Ill., 1963.

Harold R. Shurtleff. *The Log Cabin Myth.* Cambridge, Mass., 1939.

David C. Smith. *A History of Maine Lumbering, 1860–1960.* Portland, Me., 1972.

Betty Flanders Thomson. *The Changing Face of New England.* New York, 1958.

Richard G. Wood. *A History of Lumbering in Maine, 1820–1861.* Portland, Me., 1935; reprinted 1971 with new introduction.

Wood in Early American Architecture

Martin Shaw Briggs. *The Homes of the Pilgrim Fathers in England and America.* New York, 1932.

Carl W. Condit. *American Building Art: The Nineteenth Century.* New York, 1960.

James M. Fitch. *American Building: The Historical Forces That Shaped It.* Rev. ed. Boston, 1966.

John Fitchen. *The New World Dutch Barn: A Study of Its Characteristics, Its Structural System, and Its Probable Erectional Procedures.* Syracuse, N.Y., 1968.

J. Fred Kelly. *The Early Domestic Architecture of Connecticut.* New Haven, 1924.

Hugh Morrison. *Early American Architecture: From the Colonial Settlements to the National Period.* New York, 1952.

Technological Growth

Lance Davis, Richard A. Easterlin, et al. *American Economic Growth: An Economist's History of the United States.* New York, 1972.

H. J. Habakkuk. *American and British Technology in the Nineteenth Century.* Cambridge, England, 1962.

National Bureau of Economic Research. *The Rate and Direction of Inventive Activity: Economic and Social Factors.* New York, 1962.

David Pye. *Nature and Art of Workmanship.* New York, 1971.

Nathan Rosenberg. *Technology and American Economic Growth.* New York, 1972.

Nathan Rosenberg (ed.). *The American System of Manufactures.* Chicago, 1969.

W. Paul Strassmann. *Risk and Technological Innovation: American Manufacturing Methods During the Nineteenth Century.* Ithaca, N.Y., 1959.

Jacob Schmookler. *Invention and Economic Growth.* Cambridge, Mass., 1966.

Early American Artisans

Silvio Bedini. *Early American Scientific Instruments.* Washington, 1964.

Silvio Bedini. *Thinkers and Tinkers.* New York, 1974.

Carl Bridenbaugh. *The Colonial Craftsman.* New York, 1950.

I. Bernard Cohen. *Some Early Tools of Science.* Cambridge, Mass., 1950.

Charles E. Smart. *The Makers of Surveying Instruments in America since 1700.* Troy, N.Y., 1962.

Walter Muir Whitehill. *The Arts in Early American History.* Chapel Hill, N.C., 1965.

Early Milling

Greville and Dorothy Bathe. *Oliver Evans: A Chronicle of Early American Engineering.* Philadelphia, 1935.

Oliver Evans. *The Young Mill-Wright and Miller's Guide.* Philadelphia, 1795.

John Reynolds. *Windmills and Watermills.* New York, 1970.

John Storck and Walter D. Teague. *Flour for Man's Bread.* Minneapolis, 1952.

Rex Wailes. *The English Windmill.* London, 1954.

Martha and Murray Zimiles. *Early American Mills.* New York, 1973.

CONTRIBUTORS

SILVIO A. BEDINI is a historian and the Deputy Director of the National Museum of History and Technology, Smithsonian Institution. Specializing in the role of the mathematical practitioner, he has published many articles and monographs on the history of horology and of scientific instrumentation in European and American scholarly journals. Among his books are *Early American Scientific Instruments and Their Makers; Moon, Man's Greatest Adventure,* with Wernher Von Braun and Fred L. Whipple; *The Life of Benjamin Banneker,* and *Thinkers and Tinkers, Early American Men of Science.* Forthcoming publications are *From Time to Time (Historic American Timepieces)* and a monographic study on *Thomas Jefferson's Writing Devices.*

CHARLES F. CARROLL is Professor of History at the University of Lowell. He received his doctorate at Brown University where he studied under Carl Bridenbaugh. A specialist in seventeenth-century New England history, he is the author of *The Timber Economy of Puritan New England.* He is currently engaged in research on the history of the technology of early New England.

CHARLES HOWELL, a fifth-generation miller, now operates the seventeenth-century gristmill at Philipsburg Manor, North Tarrytown, New York. He came to the United States from Great Britain in 1969 to provide expert technical advice on the reconstruction of the mill. As a miller and millwright in Great Britain, he operated and repaired various types of waterpowered mills. Mr. Howell has studied early American mills extensively and often acts as a consultant on their restoration. He is an active member of the British and North American Newcomen Societies and the Society for Industrial Archaeology, as well as several other organizations devoted to the history of technology. He is presently working on an illustrated history of milling and the Philipsburg Manor gristmill.

LOUIS C. HUNTER is an economic historian, who has given particular emphasis to the role of technological factors in economic development. Beginning with the early (to 1860) Pittsburgh iron history, he moved next to western river transportation in the nineteenth century. His writings then covered the history of industrial (stationary) power, from country watermills in the late eighteenth and early nineteenth century through the early phases of the electric power industry (to 1930). A work on the latter subject is now in preparation for publication. Dr. Hunter has been associated with the undergraduate and graduate levels of instruction at a number of academic institutions and with the government.

CHARLES E. PETERSON, FAIA of Philadelphia, is an architectural historian, restorationist, and planner. After a career with the U.S. National Park Service, he retired to open an independent consulting practice. Professor Peterson investigates the technology of early American buildings and lectures at Columbia University. He organized the 1974 symposium "Building Early America" for the Carpenters' Company of Philadelphia and is now editing its book of proceedings.

NATHAN ROSENBERG is Professor of Economics at Stanford University, a rank he also held at the University of Wisconsin. He has also taught at Indiana University, University of Pennsylvania, Purdue University, Harvard University, University of the Philippines, and the London School of Economics. His major research activities have been in the history of technological change, with particular emphasis upon the forces which have shaped that change and the interrelations between technological change and economic growth. His books include *Technology and American Economic Growth*, *The American System of Manufactures*, and *The Economics of Technological Change*, which he edited. He served as editor of the *Journal of Economic History* from 1972 to 1974.

The following scholars made valuable contributions to this volume by their insightful commentaries on the papers presented at the conference on "America's Wooden Age," sponsored by Sleepy Hollow Restorations in Tarrytown, N.Y., on April 27–28, 1973.

CARL BRIDENBAUGH is Emeritus Professor of History at Brown University. He has served as Margaret Byrne Professor of History at the University of California, Berkeley, and as Director of the Institute of Early American History and Culture. He has written many books on the social history of colonial America, including *Colonial Craftsman* (1920).

EUGENE S. FERGUSON is Professor of History at the University of Delaware and Curator of Technology at the Hagley Museum, Greenville, Delaware. He holds an engineering degree from Carnegie Institute of Technology, and was for several years a practicing mechanical engineer before joining the faculty of Iowa State University. He is the author of *Bibliography of the History of Technology* and many other works.

DAVID C. SMITH is Professor of History at the University of Maine, Orono. He is a specialist in forest and agriculture history. He was trained at Cornell University and his dissertation, *A History of Maine Lumbering* 1860–1960 was published by the University of Maine press. He is also the author of several monographs, and numerous articles, as well as *A History of Paper-making in the United States* 1690–1970. He is currently writing a history of the University of Maine, and publications on the logging frontier.

The Editor

BROOKE HINDLE is Director of the National Museum of History and Technology, Smithsonian Institution. He served for many years at New York University as Professor of History, as Head of the History Department, and as Dean of University College of Arts and Sciences. Among his works on American technology are *The Pursuit of Science in Revolutionary America*, *David Rittenhouse*, and *Technology in Early America*.

INDEX